HAS THE DAY OF *miracles* CEASED?

100 TRUE LATTER-DAY MIRACLES

JONATHAN WOODSTOCK

HAS THE DAY OF *miracles* CEASED?

100 TRUE LATTER-DAY MIRACLES

CFI
AN IMPRINT OF CEDAR FORT, INC.
SPRINGVILLE, UTAH

This is not an official publication of The Church of Jesus Christ of Latter-day Saints. The opinions and views expressed herein belong solely to the author and do not necessarily represent the opinions or views of Cedar Fort, Inc. Permission for the use of sources, graphics, and photos is also solely the responsibility of the author.

ISBN 13: 978-1-4621-4175-3

Published by CFI, an imprint of Cedar Fort, Inc.
2373 W. 700 S., Springville, UT 84663
Distributed by Cedar Fort, Inc., www.cedarfort.com

Library of Congress Control Number: 2022930826

Cover design by Shawnda T. Craig

Edited and typeset by Valene Wood

Printed in the United States of America

10 9 8 7 6 5 4 3 2 1

Printed on acid-free paper

This book was written for my children, their children, and their children. They are my inspiration, but I could not have written this without the encouragement and support of my wife, Amy, and her parents, Marva and David Coombs.

Christmas 2022

Dear family, Danny, Nicole, Leah, Heston & Trey,

I read this book earlier this year and enjoyed it so much, I could hardly put it down! I hope you all enjoy it too and it helps you know that miracles are possible in our lives! If we are trying to stay on the covenant path that our prophet, Russell M Nelson, has counseled us to, it will bless our lives and we'll see more miracles, large and small, in our lives. I testify this is true! The more we make good choices, study the scriptures, and use the power of prayer to get closer to our Savior, the more miracles we will see in our lives. I grandma, am far from perfect, but I've seen many miracles in Dad and my lives and have written many down in hopes that they'll increase your testimonies as they have mine! Ask me if you wish to read them. We love you all and want you all to be healthy and happy! My experience has told me that the gospel leads us to true happiness!

Love, Chris & Janet Fuller

Contents

Introduction

Do miracles still happen today? Yes! I have seen them. I have been the recipient of them. I have listened to my family and friends recount them. I have read thousands of well-documented stories of them. I wrote this book because I am a witness that miracles like those recorded in the scriptures still occur in our day. The day of miracles has not ceased.

I have also read and listened to hundreds of secondhand, undocumented stories of miracles. They will *not* be told in this book. That doesn't mean they aren't true, but I don't want this book to be regarded as sensational or full of faith-promoting rumors. Every experience retold in this book is true and has been fully documented from credible and reliable sources.

My personal journey with modern-day miracles began forty-five years ago as a young missionary in Canada—a detailed account will be told in chapter two—but it wasn't until I became a seminary teacher for The Church of Jesus Christ of Latter-day Saints that the vastness of miraculous accounts in our day became evident. While preparing to teach about the miracles of Jesus, I found a quotation by President Spencer W. Kimball that stunned me:

> A question often asked is: "If miracles are a part of the Gospel program, why do we not have such today?" The answer is a simple one: we *do* have miracles today—beyond imagination.

> If all the miracles of our own lifetime were recorded, it would take many library shelves to hold the books which would contain them.[1]

Really? I decided to test this statement the next day in my seminary classes. I challenged my students to go home and ask their parents and other family members if they had experienced any modern-day miracles. I was shocked the next day when they came back to class and recounted dozens of personal and family stories including answers to prayers, promptings from the Holy Ghost, dreams, divine protection, priesthood blessings, and healings.

For me, the best part of that day was not the incredible stories that were told, it was the Spirit I felt. My faith in the Savior and His gospel was increased. That is why I wrote this book. I want my children and grandchildren, and anyone else who may read these stories, to be uplifted and edified by the Holy Spirit they will most certainly feel. I want their faith in God our Eternal Heavenly Father and His Son Jesus Christ to be charged. I want their testimony of the gospel of Jesus Christ to be fortified. I want their knowledge to be stretched to include the fact that miracles today attest to the power of God again on the earth.

Where did I find these amazing stories? President Kimball said we could find them, "In the records of the Church, in journals, in news and magazine articles, and in the minds and memories of many people."[2] That is where I found them. One of those magazines has turned out to be a gold mine—the *Ensign* of The Church of Jesus Christ of Latter-day Saints including the General Conference issues.

This book is *not* for unbelievers. Miracles do not create faith; you must believe first. President Brigham Young taught, "Miracles, or these extraordinary manifestations of the power of God, are not for the unbeliever; they are to console the Saints, and to strengthen and confirm the faith of those who love, fear, and serve God."[3] Although, the vast majority of the miraculous accounts I recorded are about members of The Church of Jesus Christ of Latter-day Saints, I do

1. "The Significance of Miracles in the Church Today," *Instructor*, Dec. 1959, 396.
2. Ibid.
3. *Journal of Discourses*, 26 vols. (London: Latter-day Saints' Book Depot, 1854–86), 12:97.

not believe that only members of the Church should read this book. Anyone with a sincere heart and faith in God and His Son Jesus Christ may benefit—just remember that faith comes first.

Another forewarning: this book is not a commentary about ancient miracles recorded in the scriptures. Many capable authors have already contributed much to that subject.[4] My purpose is to create a straightforward, readable book about latter-day miracles that my children and grandchildren will enjoy.

The first chapter teaches about miracles in general, what they are, why miracles are needed today, how they are produced, and the indispensable role of faith. The next ten chapters give examples of ten different kinds of miracles: promptings from the Holy Ghost, answers to prayer, fasting and prayer, administration to the sick, divine protection, sacred dreams, miracles in nature, healing physical infirmities, unique miracles, and power over death. This is not a complete list of types of miracles, but enough for a first volume. I purposely placed the most common kinds of miracles found today first and chose to end with those types of miracles that are extremely rare. The concluding chapters address two important subjects: what our response should be when miracles don't happen, and what our responsibility is as recipients of these marvelous manifestations.

I testify that miracles are as much a part of the gospel of Jesus Christ today as baptism, prayer, and the sacrament. The power of God is still manifest today. Miracles will continue among the Lord's people, "so long as time shall last, or the earth shall stand, or there shall be one man upon the face thereof to be saved" (Moroni 7:36).

4. Recent examples from Latter-day Saint authors include Alonzo L. Gaskill's *Miracles of the New Testament* and Eric D. Huntsman's *The Miracles of Jesus*.

Chapter 1

He Is a God of Miracles

"God has not ceased to be a God of miracles."
Mormon 9:15

---

1 *Don't Start the Car!*

When Gun Wastlund first stepped into his car, he had an uneasy feeling. Something was wrong. He looked out the windows and into his rearview mirror; he couldn't see anything wrong. He was already late for work, so he put his keys into the ignition.

"Don't start the car."

This time it wasn't just a bad feeling; it was like a voice spoke inside his mind.

"What?" Gun thought, "Why shouldn't I start the car?"

He opened his car door and looked up and down the driveway—nothing. "This is silly," he thought. "I've got to get to work." He reached one more time for his keys.

"Don't start the car!"

The impression was much stronger and clearer now. He later described it as a loud voice compelling him not to start the car. There had to be something wrong. Gun opened the door and walked around the car to make a visual inspection. He didn't see anything, so he got down on his hands and knees and looked underneath the car. He was shocked to find a small boy sound asleep, curled up next to his right rear tire. He was the next-door neighbor's three-year-old "Dennis the Menace," a kid who was always in trouble. Gun pulled the boy from underneath the car and returned him to his home.

When he finally left for work, Gun was shaken but grateful that he had listened to the impressions of the Spirit. He had participated in a modern-day miracle.[1]

WHAT IS A MIRACLE?

Was Gun's miracle divine providence or a lucky coincidence? That depends on who defines what a miracle is. My worn-out, paperback American Heritage dictionary defined a miracle as, "a combination of accidental circumstances that seems to have been planned or arranged." Are you kidding me? Are we supposed to believe that Gun accidentally heard a voice telling him not to start the car at the exact moment a child was sleeping underneath his car?

Contrast that definition with a latter-day prophet of God: miracles are "extraordinary manifestations of the power of God."[2]

President Howard W. Hunter put it this way: "Among the signs of the true church, and included in the evidences of God's work in the world, are the manifestations of his power which we are helpless to explain or fully understand."[3]

Miracles are sometimes hard to explain or to fully understand. Cell phone technology is difficult for me to understand. How in the world is it possible for my voice, with its exact tone and pitch, to be heard instantly 6,000 miles away? Yet, there are people who do understand how that marvel works. Could not the same be said for spiritual miracles? It would be egotistical to think that just because I don't understand how Gun Wastlund was miraculously warned, that nobody else, particularly God, could understand it either.

Try to explain this modern miracle.

---

1. Personal Interview recorded with the author on February 14, 2016. Gun Wastlund is the father of my oldest daughter's husband. He is also the "other" grandfather to six of my grandchildren.
2. *Journal of Discourses*, 26 vols. (London: Latter-day Saints' Book Depot, 1854–86), 12:97.
3. "The God That Doest Wonders," April 1989 General Conference, *Ensign*, May 1989, 15.

2 Have You Ever Seen This Book?

No one sat next to Steven McLaws on his flight from Omaha to Houston, so he left the Book of Mormon on the seat next to him when he got off the plane. He traveled frequently, and he usually tried to discuss the gospel with the person sitting next to him. If possible, he gave him or her a copy of the Book of Mormon.

Two weeks later, he flew from Omaha to Los Angeles and was again ready to place a Book of Mormon. He was surprised when the man seated next to him pulled a book out from his briefcase and said, "Have you ever seen this book?" It was a Book of Mormon.

The stranger explained, "I picked it up a couple of weeks ago in Houston as I was boarding a flight to San Antonio. Someone wrote something about the book in the front and included his phone number, but he didn't put the area code, so I haven't been able to call him."

Steven said, "Let me see that book."

He opened it and saw his own handwritten testimony written in the front. He took a pen out of his pocket, added the area code to his telephone number, and handed the book back to the man.

They stared at each other in awe for several moments. Steven's new friend had read about a third of the Book of Mormon in the last two weeks. They spent the remainder of the flight discussing their feelings about the Book of Mormon. Steven later introduced him to the full-time missionaries.[4]

4. "'A powerful convincer': Book of Mormon, missionary tool for all lands," *Church News*, Jan. 2, 1988.

THE WORLD'S VIEW OF MIRACLES

I was surprised to learn that 72% of Americans believe that God still performs miracles today. Almost half of those said they had experienced miracles themselves.[5]

Why then do so many Christian churches today teach that miracles stopped the first century after Christ? One Protestant minister explained his reasoning:

> Since the purpose of miraculous gifts has been fulfilled, to reveal and confirm the truth, these gifts have ceased. . . . Also, the means of obtaining the miraculous gifts has ceased. Only the apostles had the ability, by the laying on of hands, to pass the gifts of the Spirit to another Christian. No apostles are living today to perform these signs, or to impart these gifts; . . . Likewise, there is no one living today who has received a miraculous gift from an apostle. Thus, when the last apostle died and the last person upon whom the apostles had laid hands died, there was no one who could perform miracles![6]

This preacher had the right idea; it does take authority by the laying on of hands to obtain "the means of obtaining miraculous gifts." But what he doesn't understand is that the authority *has* been restored to the earth, and that there are once again living prophets and apostles.

The prophet Mormon asked a great question: "If there were miracles wrought then [when Jesus and His apostles were on the earth], why has God ceased to be a God of miracles and yet be an unchangeable Being?" (Mormon 9:19). Isn't God supposed to be the same "yesterday, today, and forever?" (2 Nephi 27:23).[7]

I testify that God has not ceased to be God. His priesthood authority has been restored to the earth through the Prophet Joseph Smith. Living prophets and apostles again have the keys to bestow

5. Larry Shannon-Missal, "Americans' Belief in God, Miracles and Heaven Declines," *The Harris Poll*, Dec. 16, 2013. https://theharrispoll.com/new-york-n-y-december-16-2013.
6. Donny Weimar, "Modern Day Miracles: Are They Fact Or Fiction?" *The Old Paths Archive*, 1969, https://oldpaths.com/Archive/Weimar/Donny/W/1969/miracles.html.
7. See also Hebrews 13:8 and Moroni 10:19.

priesthood authority, which brings the power of modern-day miracles. "God has provided a means that man, through faith, might work mighty miracles" (Mosiah 8:18).

3 *A Day of God's Power*

Early members of The Church of Jesus Christ of Latter-day Saints had been driven from New York, then Ohio, and then Missouri. Now mosquitos were threatening to do the same in Illinois. Those who weren't sick were nursing those who were.

Brother Joseph, as everyone called the prophet Joseph Smith, had opened his home and yard to the sick and dying. He had waited on them until he was worn out. Keep in mind that Joseph had just returned from seven months of miserable confinement in three different Missouri jails. He'd had enough.

Wilford Woodruff called July 22, 1839, "A Day of God's Power." It was that morning when the Prophet Joseph Smith called upon God in fervent prayer, and "the power of God rested upon him mightily."

He healed all those who were stricken ill inside his home and yard; then taking with him several of the apostles, went among the sick laid by the river. "He commanded them in a loud voice, in the name of Jesus Christ, to rise and be made whole, and they were all healed," testified Wilford.

The prophet of God then crossed the Mississippi River in a ferryboat to the Mormon settlement of Montrose. He found the senior apostle Brigham Young sick in bed. He healed him, and then Brigham joined the group.

They went to Elijah Fordham's house. He was clearly dying; those with him expected his last breath at any moment.

"I felt the Spirit of God that was overpowering His Prophet," said Wilford. Joseph removed his hat when he entered the room and held it in his left hand. He walked up to Elijah, took him by the right hand and looked into his eyes. They were glazed like glass beads in his head; he lay unconscious, unaware of anyone around him. Joseph continued to hold his hand and stare into his eyes for a length of time.

Then, those in the room noticed a change in the dying man's countenance. He looked at Joseph, who said, "Brother Fordham, do you not know me?"

There was no reply, but everyone could feel the Spirit of God resting on him.

"Elijah, do you not know me?"

In a low whisper, Brother Fordham replied, "Yes."

"Have you not faith to be healed?"

"I am afraid it is too late; if you had come sooner, I think I might have been," Elijah said with a little more strength. Wilford later said, "He had the appearance of a man waking from . . . the sleep of death."

Joseph then said, "Do you believe that Jesus is the Christ?"

"I do, Brother Joseph."

The Prophet stood erect, still holding Brother Fordham's hand. He was silent for a few moments and then spoke with a loud voice, "Elijah, I command you, in the name of Jesus of Nazareth, to arise and be made whole."

Wilford wrote that he spoke "as in the majesty of Jehovah. . . . [T]he words of the Prophet were not like the words of man, but like the voice of God. It seemed to me that the house shook on its foundation."

"Elijah Fordham leaped from his bed like a man raised from the dead," testified Wilford. "A healthy color came to his face, and life was manifested in every act." He dressed, ate a bowl of bread and milk, and then followed the group into the street to visit others who were sick.[8]

---

8. Matthias F. Cowley, *Wilford Woodruff: History of His Life and Labors*, 104–105. Also see Joseph Fielding Smith, *Essentials in Church History,* rev. ed. Salt Lake City: Deseret Book, 1979, 223–24.

WHY ARE MIRACLES STILL NEEDED TODAY?

Indeed, the God of miracles is not dead. The gospel of Jesus Christ has been restored to the earth with His priesthood holding the keys to perform miracles in all varieties, but why? Why are miracles still necessary in the latter days? Here are some possible reasons to think about:

1. To witness there is a God.[9]
2. To testify that God still performs miracles.[10]
3. To show that God has all power.[11]
4. To give us hope.[12]
5. To symbolize God's power to heal us not only physically but spiritually also.
6. To witness that priesthood power is again on the earth.
7. To allow us to help and benefit other people.[13]
8. To open the hearts of unbelievers.
9. To show that God, when necessary, can and will intercede in our lives.
10. To witness to the world that the true church of God is again on the earth.[14]

On a personal level, an important question to ask yourselves is: Why do I need to know, right now in my life, that miracles still occur every day? I asked that question to my oldest daughter Amber, and she replied,

> It will take a miracle for us of this generation to escape the evils of the world and rise triumphant at the last day. If the day of miracles has ceased, so has faith. I hold true to the hope that if I remain faithful, my Savior will shower miracles upon me and my family in our greatest need. We will be surprised when we reach the other side of the veil how many miracles actually occurred in our lives to help us fulfill our missions upon this earth.

---

9. Psalms 77:14.
10. 2 Nephi 27:23.
11. Doctrine and Covenants 35:8.
12. Eric D. Huntsman, *The Miracles of Jesus* (Salt Lake City: Deseret Book, 2014), 7.
13. Mosiah 8:18.
14. Bruce R. McConkie, *Mormon Doctrine*, 2nd ed. (Salt Lake City: Bookcraft, 1966), 507.

I then asked Amber what miracles she had experienced in her life. She shared with me three experiences from her childhood that I had no knowledge of until then. She said, "I think of you and Mom as parents, and how you weren't even aware of the many miracles that were occurring to protect your family. I pray that the same miracles are occurring in the lives of my own children." Let me share with you one of the small miracles she shared with me.

4 Go Get Katie

Many years ago, we owned a Ford Ranger pickup with a topper, and something called a "carpet kit." It slid in the back of the pickup so our small children could play or sleep comfortably while traveling. Seat belts were optional in those days, and we saw no particular danger. There was a sliding glass window from the cab of the truck, so we could communicate with the children.

My daughters Amber and Katie, ages ten and two at the time, were riding in the back. Amber sat with her back against the cab of the truck, facing the rear. Katie sat opposite leaning against the tailgate.

Suddenly, Amber had a very strong impression: "Go get Katie." She looked at her little sister and wondered why, when almost instantly she heard again, "Go get Katie!"

She felt a great urgency and went and grabbed her, pulling her near the cab of the truck. A few moments later the truck went over a bump, and the tailgate flew open. Had Katie been sitting there, she would have fallen out and most likely have been run over by the cars behind us.[15]

As a father, I am grateful for the many miracles that have protected my family even without my knowledge at the time.

15. E-mail communication on February 29, 2016.

THE ROLE OF FAITH

Let's think about Amber's story a little more. What if she had ignored the voice believing it was just her imagination? For any miracle to work, there must be faith. Perhaps that is why Jesus referred to His own miracles as "works" (John 10:32).

A scriptural word for "work" is "wrought." "[A]ll they who *wrought* miracles *wrought* them by faith," wrote the prophet Moroni shortly before burying the plates. "And neither at any time hath any *wrought* miracles until after their faith; wherefore they first believed in the Son of God" (Ether 12:16, 18,emphasis added).

Another of the keywords in that verse needs to be emphasized—"first." You must *first* believe, and then miracles follow.[16] Miracles do not create faith. In fact, sometimes the opposite happens. Jesus made enemies because of the miracles He performed, as did many of the prophets.

Look at Nephi, the son of Nephi, who later became one of the Savior's apostles. About the same time Jesus was performing mighty miracles throughout Galilee and Judea, the prophet Nephi was also performing mighty miracles in the western hemisphere. What kind of miracles did Nephi perform? The same as Jesus—devils cast out, healing of the sick and infirm, "and even his brother did he raise from the dead" (3 Nephi 7:17–22).

Were all the Nephites converted because of the wonderful miracles Nephi performed? No! "And the people saw it, and did witness of it, and were angry with him because of his power" (3 Nephi 7:20).

How is it possible to witness someone being raised from the dead and not be instantly convinced? They did not have faith *first*. Here is a modern example.

16. See Mark 16:17.

5 *It Is the Power of God That Has Healed You*

Most little boys like climbing trees. James Peck certainly did. Unfortunately, he lost his balance and fell out of the tree, breaking his arm.

Dr. Harvey Tate just happened to be visiting with James's father at the very moment he came screaming into the house. It was painfully obvious the arm was broken. Even if an x-ray machine had been invented at that point in time, one did not need an x-ray to see that the arm just a few inches above the wrist was not supposed to bend at a right angle.

Dr. Tate set the bone and bandaged it. There was no anesthesia or pain medicine to give him. The country doctor did all he could do. James was put to bed and Dr. Tate left.

The boy was still in agonizing pain though; he didn't know how he could endure it. James begged his father to give him a priesthood blessing, expressing his faith in God's ability to heal him.

Martin Peck had only been a member of the Church a short time, but he too had faith in the power of God's holy priesthood. He laid his hands upon his son and blessed him. The pain immediately ceased.

James slept well throughout the night. The next morning, he was playing with his friends as if nothing had ever happened. Martin sent him to the doctor's house to have him look at his arm.

Dr. Tate was surprised when James picked up a chair with his injured arm and brought it forward to sit with. He carefully examined his arm, had James wiggle his fingers, and move about his wrist.

He asked, "Do you feel any pain?"

"No," replied the boy.

"It is the power of God that has healed you," Dr. Tate declared, "Nothing else could have done it in so short a time."

He was convinced that the Latter-day Saints could perform miracles and was soon baptized.[17]

FAITH FIRST

In this story, Dr. Tate did not believe until after he saw the miracle. What's wrong with that? There was no foundation to build upon. "The viewing of signs or miracles is not a secure foundation for conversion," said President Dallin H. Oaks. "Scriptural history attests that people converted by signs and wonders soon forget them and again become susceptible to the lies and distortions of Satan and his servants."[18]

That is exactly what happened to the doctor. He was baptized in 1836 in Kirtland, Ohio after seeing James Peck's arm healed and was active in the Church for a short time, but when adversity came, he did not have the faith to continue.

Primary children love to sing, "The wise man built his house upon the rock." I testify that the rock is Jesus the Christ. When we build our foundation of testimony upon Him and His gospel, we will have a sure foundation from which we cannot fall when "the rains come tumbling down."[19]

---

17. "Remarkable Healings," *Early Scenes in Church History* (Salt Lake City: Juvenile Instructor Office, 1882), 72–73. Also found in the family history of Martin Horton Peck written by Vernice Peck Gold Rosenvall, https://familysearch.org/photos/stories/35550.
18. Dallin H. Oaks, *The Lord's Way*, (Salt Lake City: Deseret Book, 1991), 87.
19. "The Wise Man and the Foolish Man," *Children's Songbook*, 281.

Chapter 2

Promptings from the Holy Ghost

"The voice of the Lord came into my mind."
Enos 1:10

6 Get Out from under This Car

The young man nervously stepped to the pulpit to bear his testimony. He felt compelled to stand and share with the congregation what had happened to him less than twenty-four hours earlier.

"I was out working on my car yesterday. All of a sudden something seemed to say to me, 'Get out from under this car!' I did, and instantly the car dropped down off the supports I had it resting on. I know I would have been crushed to death. I'm so grateful to my Heavenly Father for watching over me."[1]

RECEIVING THE GIFT OF THE HOLY GHOST

Every member of the Lord's church must obtain the first two ordinances of the gospel—baptism and laying on of hands for the gift of the Holy Ghost. *Receiving* the gift of the Holy Ghost is optional.

1. Jay Parry, "Miracles Today?" *Ensign*, July 1978.

What? Wasn't I told at my confirmation to "receive the Holy Ghost?"

That's right; you were told to receive it. Did you? Are you still receiving it?

Agency is one of the most precious gifts Heavenly Father has given. He gave it to us before we even came to this earth. We exercised that agency when we told our bishop, or the missionaries, that we desired to be baptized.

That agency must also be exercised when the Holy Priesthood commands us to receive the Holy Ghost. The Bible Dictionary in the Latter-day Saint edition of the King James version states, "The gift of the Holy Ghost is the *right* to have, whenever one is worthy, the companionship of the Holy Ghost."[2] Notice the word "right." The Holy Ghost is not obligated to perform his functions for us if we choose not to receive him. We choose to receive him when we strive to live worthily. I added the word "strive" because we don't have to be perfect to have the constant companionship of the Holy Ghost; we have to be trying.[3]

I had a horrible dream one night many years ago that my oldest son, Jamen, then just a small child, had his foot cut off. That was not the worst part of the dream for me though. I dreamed that I was not worthy to lay my hands upon my son and bless him. I had no power to make him better. I was so happy when I awoke and realized it had been a terrible nightmare.

The same is true of receiving promptings from the gift of the Holy Ghost. We cannot expect the Holy Ghost to prompt us when we are purposefully disobeying the Father's commandments. From the very beginning of the holy scriptures, we are told, "My spirit shall not always strive with man" (Genesis 6:3).

My first wife Vickie was not perfect, but she was constantly repenting, changing, and trying her best to live the commandments. Here is a story from her young adult years that show the Holy Ghost is anxious and willing to assist even imperfect people.

---

2. Bible Dictionary, "Holy Ghost," 704, emphasis added.
3. See Elder Bruce R. McConkie's "The Probationary Test of Mortality," address delivered at Institute of Religion, SLC, Utah, 10 Jan. 1982.

7 Watch That Kid

Vickie worked as a lifeguard every summer at Falcon swimming pool. It was a small community pool run by the city of Mesa, Arizona. When it was first built, the pool was located quite a distance from any homes; eventually the orange groves were torn down as the city sprawled into the desert. There were days when only a handful of people, mostly children, would come to swim. Sometimes parents would use the pool as a babysitter and drop their children off for the entire day.

One afternoon Vickie opened the pool and set out the small cash drawer. Usually, there were two lifeguards assigned, one to run the cash register, and the other to watch the people in the pool. For some reason, the other lifeguard was not there that day. However, with only a small number of children expected, she could still watch the pool while also running the cash register.

A small girl reached for Vickie's hand. "Hi," she said. Vickie smiled and took her money, but as the girl entered into the pool area, the Spirit whispered to her, "Watch that kid."

Sure enough, later in the day, the little girl went into the deep end of the pool. Vickie could see immediately that she did not know how to swim. She jumped in to get her. Vickie then admonished the little girl to stay in the shallow end of the pool.

Five minutes later, Vickie was helping some new customers when she turned around to make sure everything was OK in the pool. She looked specifically for "that kid." A quick glance over the small pool was all she needed to notice that the little girl was nowhere in sight. Then she spotted her—at the bottom of the pool.

She screamed, "Everybody out of the pool," while simultaneously diving into the deep end. When she pulled the girl out and laid her on the deck of the pool, she was not breathing. Vickie immediately began mouth-to-mouth resuscitation.

Vickie wrote in her personal journal that night, "Thanks to God, not to me, she began breathing again. Her coughing was the most wonderful sound I had ever heard. I was quite shook up for the rest of the day. The Spirit has helped me so much at the pool. I love the Lord so much; He helps me every day."[4]

THE HOLY GHOST IS A REVELATOR

The Holy Ghost has many roles or functions. Consider the following list. This is not a complete list, or in any particular order:

- He testifies of truth (John 15:26; D&C 100:8).
- He helps us discern the thoughts or intents of others (Alma 12:3; 18:16).
- He comforts (John 14:26; D&C 88:3).
- He allows a person to speak with authority and boldness (1 Nephi 10:22; Moroni 8:16).
- He gives truth and knowledge (John 16:13; D&C 6:14; 11:13–14).
- He brings things to our remembrance (John 14:26).
- He can show us what to do (2 Nephi 32:5; D&C 28:15).
- He can inspire us in what we should say (Luke 12:11–12; D&C 84:85; 100:5–6).
- He brings sanctification and remission of sins (Alma 13:12; 3 Nephi 27:20).
- He carries the truth to the hearts of people (2 Nephi 33:1; Alma 24:8).
- He sometimes constrains or restrains us (1 Nephi 7:15; 2 Nephi 28:1; 32:7; Alma 14:11).
- He gives "gifts of the Spirit" (1 Cor. 12:1–11; Moroni 10:8–17; D&C 46:11–26).
- He warns of danger (Alma 48:15–16; see section later in this chapter).
- He is a revelator (Alma 9:21; D&C 34:10).

The prophet Joseph Smith said, "No man can receive the Holy Ghost without receiving revelations. The Holy Ghost is a revelator."[5]

---

4. Vickie Church Woodstock is the author's first wife. She died October 11, 2012. This experience happened July 1, 1978 and is recorded in her journal.
5. *History of the Church*, 6:58; from a discourse given by Joseph Smith on Oct. 15, 1843.

So in essence, all the above functions and roles of the Holy Ghost can be summed up in the statement, "The Holy Ghost is a revelator."

Joseph Smith later taught John Taylor, "Now, if you will continue to follow the leadings of that Spirit, it will always lead you right. Sometimes it might be contrary to your judgment; never mind that, follow its dictates; and if you be true to its whisperings it will in time become in you a *principle of revelation* so that you will know all things."[6]

The next two stories illustrate two people who wondered at first if their judgment was right, but who chose to follow the promptings of the Holy Ghost.

8 *Bear Her Testimony in Portuguese*

Gayle Clegg learned to speak Portuguese when her family lived in Brazil; her husband Calvin worked there for two years. He was later called as a mission president to Portugal and Gayle served by his side.

In 1999, Gayle was called as the second counselor in the Primary general presidency of The Church of Jesus Christ of Latter-day Saints.[7] In that capacity, she traveled to meet with the Latter-day Saints in Japan in 2003.

Gayle was surprised to see a Brazilian family in the chapel where she was scheduled to speak. "They just looked Brazilian," she said.

Her talk was given in English, while a translator spoke in Japanese. At the end of her message, Gayle felt impressed to bear her testimony in Portuguese. She hesitated, knowing there would be no Portuguese translators, and most of the people would not understand her, but she obeyed the prompting from the Holy Ghost.

The Brazilian father came up to her after the meeting and said, "Sister, the customs are so different here, and I have been lonely. It is difficult to come to church and not understand anything. Sometimes I wonder if I would be better off just

6. John Taylor, *Deseret News: Semi-Weekly*, Jan. 15, 1878, 1, emphasis added.
7. Latter-day Saints refer to their children's organization as Primary.

reading my scriptures at home. I told my wife, I'll give it one more chance, and I came today for what I thought was the last time. When you bore your testimony in Portuguese, the Spirit touched my heart, and I knew that this is where I belonged. God knows I am here, and He will help me."

Think about the chances of that entire experience. A family leaves their home in Brazil, travels 11,000 miles to Japan, finds an American woman who has traveled 6,000 miles and just happens to know their language. When that story was told in the General Conference of the church, the Primary General President Sydney Reynolds wondered, "Was it a coincidence that the only Portuguese-speaking member of the Primary presidency was sent to Japan instead of to Portugal? Or was it because the Lord knew someone there needed what only she could give—and she had the courage to follow a prompting of the Spirit?"[8]

9 No Way to Contact Her Home Teacher

An elderly woman in England knelt down to pray. She had just come from the doctor's office where she learned she had cancer. The doctor told her she must decide whether to be operated on or let nature take its course. As she prayed, she felt impressed to ask her home teacher to help her decide. She had no telephone, however, so she prayed that Brother Hales would come by to see her.

Robert D. Hales, an executive for a cosmetic company, got a strong feeling while at work that he needed to visit one of the sisters he home taught.

He called his wife to tell her he would be late getting home. She reminded him they were having a dinner party that night. "I know," he said, "I'll get there as soon as I can." Mary Hales understood. "I had learned a long time ago to not stand in the way when Bob has an impression he should go somewhere or call someone," she said.

8. Sydney S. Reynolds, "He Knows Us; He Loves Us," *Ensign*, November 2003, 76.

Brother Hales visited with the elderly sister. They prayed together, and she decided to let nature take its course. She died a few weeks later. "The doctors said the operation would have done her absolutely no good," Mary Hales said. "I thought, 'What if I had said something to Bob about coming straight home, that we had obligations to our guests?'"[9]

It was only a few years later that Robert D. Hales, the home teacher, was called as Elder Robert D. Hales, a General Authority of The Church of Jesus Christ of Latter-day Saints. He would go on to serve as the Presiding Bishop of the Church, and as a member of the Quorum of the Twelve Apostles. Perhaps one of the reasons he was called was because he had learned early in his life to listen to the promptings of the Holy Ghost.

WARNINGS OF DANGER

The prophet Lehi was warned to take his family and flee the city of Jerusalem (1 Nephi 2:2); Nephi was warned to separate his people from Laman and Lemuel (2 Nephi 5:5); Noah was warned that a flood would come upon the world (Genesis 6:13–17).

The following five short stories are latter-day examples of people who were warned through inspiration from the Holy Ghost. As you read their accounts, look for the different ways the promptings came: "I felt impressed," "I heard a voice in my mind," "I felt strongly impressed." President Boyd K. Packer said, "The Holy Ghost communicates with the spirit through the mind more than through the physical senses. This guidance comes as thoughts, as feelings, through impressions and promptings. It is not always easy to describe inspiration. The scriptures teach us that we may 'feel' the words of spiritual communication more than hear them."[10] A friend of mine described it as a squeezing of the heart.

9. Gerry Avant, "New apostle aware of heightened role," *Church News*, April 16, 1994.
10. Boyd K. Packer, "Revelation in a Changing World," *Ensign*, Nov. 1989, 14.

10 *Don't Go Aboard That Steamer*

Wilford Woodruff, future President of the Church, served many full-time missions for the Lord. During one to the Eastern United States, he had been commissioned to gather the recent converts and bring them to Utah. When they got to Pittsburgh, the company of one-hundred Latter-day Saints was spared from disaster because he listened to the voice of the Spirit.

They arrived at sundown, and Wilford saw that a steamboat was getting ready to leave. He talked to the captain about the possibility of his company gaining passage on his ship.

"How many passengers do you have?"

"Three hundred and fifty," replied the captain.

"Could you take another hundred?"

"Yes."

Just then, the Spirit said to Wilford, "Don't go aboard that steamer; you nor your company."

Wilford Woodruff had learned to recognize and to be obedient to the Spirit's warning voice, so they decided to wait until the next morning and find another boat.

Five miles down the river, the first steamer caught fire. Three hundred persons were burned to death or drowned. Wilford and his company safely traveled on another boat the next day.[11]

11 *Now Wasn't That Silly of Me*

Boyd Kenneth Packer grew up on a small farm in northern Utah. His parents taught him by example the principles of the gospel like faith and listening to the promptings of the Holy Ghost.

One morning his father Ira broke a plow. He came in from the field, and said to his wife, "I must go to Brigham City and get some welding done. Would you like to go?"

Emma Packer had much to do—it was washing day—but she did need to go to the store, so she quickly set things

---

11. Wilford Woodruff, *The Discourses of Wilford Woodruff*, sel. G. Homer Durham (Salt Lake City: Bookcraft, 1946), 294–95.

aside and began to get the smaller children ready for a trip into town.

She and the children met Ira at the front gate as he pulled up the horse and buggy. As she put her foot onto the step of the carriage, she had an impression. She paused. "Dad, somehow I feel I shouldn't go with you today."

"But why not? Hurry, time is wasting. You know you have shopping to do."

Emma finally said, "I just feel like I shouldn't go."

Boyd's father did not push anymore. "If you feel that way, Mother, perhaps you should stay home."

As her husband drove away, Emma stood there pondering. She said to herself, "Now wasn't that silly of me?"

She returned to her chores, but only a few minutes later she smelled smoke. Emma went throughout the house looking for the source. Suddenly, the ceiling of their bedroom burst into flame; a rusted stovepipe had permitted a spark to fall and settle in the ceiling. She and the children quickly hauled in buckets of water from the back pump, and the fire was soon extinguished.

When Elder Boyd K. Packer told that story about his parents in one of his first general conference talks, he made an interesting comment: "The incident closes without significance, unless you ask the question, 'Why didn't she go to town that day?'"[12]

12 Get Out of Here

The world's most active volcano is Kilauea, located on the big island of Hawaii. Since the early 1800s, visitors have been fascinated with its almost constant activity. It has made the news in recent years because the lava flow has increased, has destroyed two hundred homes, and has added new coastline to the island. Kilauea has a large summit caldera with a central crater. According to Hawaiian legends, it is the home of the fire goddess Pele. Until 1924, it contained a lava lake.

12. Boyd L. Packer, in Conference Report, Oct. 1962, 49.

One day in 1921, David O. McKay, then a young apostle, took a night trip to see Kilauea with several other leaders and missionaries from the Church. They stood on the rim of the volcano and looked down into the "fiery pit." Although the lava lake was a hundred feet below, they could feel the intense heat of the volcanic activity.

There was a cool stiff wind at their back which soon chilled them a little too much. One of the missionaries noticed there was a ledge about four feet below the rim where you could stand away from the wind and have a better view of the volcano.

After testing the ledge for safety, four of them climbed down to it from the rim. The view was spectacular. They spent a considerable amount of time there transfixed by the glow of lava against the night sky.

Suddenly Elder McKay said, "Brethren, I feel impressed that we should get out of here." He quickly helped the other three climb back to the rim. They in turn pulled him out. Almost immediately, the entire balcony crumbled and fell into the molten lava below.

Without saying a word to each other, they stood dumbfounded as they contemplated what their awful fate might have been. None of them ever doubted "the reality of revelation in our day!"[13]

13 Get the Children Out of the Riverbed

Chasty Olsen, a young girl from Castle Dale, Utah, was watching some children play in the riverbed one day. Suddenly she heard a voice, "Chasty. Get the children out of the riverbed."

She looked up at the clear blue sky. "It isn't going to rain," she thought, so she ignored the impression.

Urgently, the voice spoke again, "Chasty! Get the children out of the riverbed!"

This time Chasty obeyed. No sooner had they reached the safety of the bank, than an enormous wall of water swept

13. *Cherished Experiences from the Writings of David O. McKay*, compiled by Clare Middlemiss (Salt Lake City: Deseret Book, 1940), 55–56.

down the canyon where the children had been playing. A cloudburst in the mountains above Castle Dale had released the sudden torrent.[14]

Chasty later married and had children of her own, one of whom became the mother of an apostle, President Dallin H. Oaks.

14 *Don't Open the Door*

A winter storm raged outside, but Janet was safe and warm inside her home with her children sound asleep. Her husband was at a bishopric meeting at the chapel. She was surprised to hear a knock at their front door at 8:30 p.m. "Immediately I felt strongly impressed that I was not to open the door." She had never felt a warning of danger like that before.

"Who's there?" Janet called through the door.

"Michael," came the reply.

It was her brother-in-law, her husband's only brother. Janet was surprised that she should feel danger. They had a good relationship with Michael, and he came often to visit. She obeyed the warning though and asked him to meet with his brother up at the chapel.

After a moment of silence, Michael spoke through the door in a strange manner explaining how he had come by train and bus to get here. The snow was getting deep and he was cold standing on their doorstep.

"A powerful prompting continued to impress upon me that I must not, for any reason, open the door." Janet calmly explained that she was sorry and repeated her request for him to go to the chapel.

He left, and Janet pondered why she had turned her brother-in-law away. "How could anyone be so uncaring? Yet at the same time I was unable to deny the strong witness that I was in danger and must not open my door." She went to bed.

14. Dallin H. Oaks, "Revelation," Brigham Young University devotional, Sept. 29, 1981, speeches.byu.edu; "Eight Reasons for Revelation," *Ensign*, Sept. 2004.

When her husband came home from his meeting, Michael came with him and was given a place to sleep downstairs.

The next morning Janet wondered how she would explain her actions. Would he be upset? When she walked into the kitchen, Michael was smiling at her. "I'm so glad you did not let us in last night," he said.

"Us?" Janet thought to herself. She had thought he was alone.

Michael proceeded to tell them how he had met Steve, an old school friend, on the train. He was high on drugs. His friend became more and more aggressive during the journey. He explained he urgently needed money and a place to sleep. He forcibly accompanied Michael to his brother's home with "the most evil of intentions."

"So, you see," said Michael, "I stood outside the door, praying that you would not let us in. By the time we set off on the long trip to the chapel, Steve lost interest and said he would go and find some 'action' somewhere else."

Janet was so grateful she had obeyed the prompting of danger sent from the Holy Ghost, even though there had been no logical reason at the time.[15]

FOR THE BENEFIT OF OTHERS

I had a startling insight as I edited the stories for this chapter. It occurred to me that all but one of the stories had the same conclusion: the prompting people received was for the benefit of others, and not specifically for them. This provoked me to examine the other stories throughout the other chapters. It was the same. I thought of one of the verses describing gifts of the Spirit—special endowments given to those who have received the gift of the Holy Ghost: "And all these gifts come from God, for the benefit of the children of God" (Doctrine and Covenants 46:26). They are given not just for our benefit, but also to bless the lives of others.

President Thomas S. Monson is a perfect example of this principle.

15. Janet Dunne, "Don't Open the Door!" *Ensign*, January 2006, 68–69.

15 *He Had Been Calling My Name*

Thomas S. Monson had learned as a young bishop never to discount a prompting from the Spirit. He learned that lesson when he ignored a prompting to visit a member of his ward in the hospital. When he finally did go, the member had already died. He vowed that night to always listen to and obey the Spirit.[16]

While serving as a counselor to President Gordon B. Hinckley, President Monson was taking care of business in his office one day, when a strong impression came to visit one of "his widows." Without hesitation, President Monson dropped everything he was doing and drove to the senior care facility where this woman was being cared for. During his service as a bishop on the west side of Salt Lake City many years before, there had been eighty-six widows. It was shortly after the Second World War, and Bishop Monson had felt a heavy responsibility to watch over them. When he was released as bishop, he continued to visit them and spoke at most of their funerals.[17]

When President Monson arrived at the senior care facility, her room was empty. Someone directed him to the lounge where she was visiting with family. As he was talking to them, a man came into the room to get a drink from the vending machine. He looked at President Monson in surprise. "Why, you are Tom Monson."

"Yes," President Monson replied, "And you look like a Hemingway." The man introduced himself as the son of Gene Hemingway, who had served as a counselor to Bishop Monson over fifty years previously. Gene was now a patient at the same facility and was near death.

"He had been calling my name," President Monson later said. The family had wanted to contact President Monson but had been unable to find a telephone number for him. President

16. Jeffrey R. Holland, "President Thomas S. Monson: Man of Action, Man of Faith, Always 'on the Lord's Errand,'" *Ensign*, Feb. 1986, 11.
17. Marianne Holman Prescott, "As a young bishop, Thomas S. Monson cared for 85 widows," *Church News*, Jan. 3, 2018.

Monson immediately excused himself and went to Gene's room. All the children were gathered to witness their father's passing. "We gave a blessing to him," President Monson recalled. "A spirit of peace prevailed. We had a lovely visit, after which I left." Twenty minutes later, Gene passed away. The family members regarded finding President Monson in the lounge area as providential. He told the members of the Church at general conference, "I, too, felt that this was the case, for if Stephen had not entered the room in which I was visiting at precisely the time he did, I would not have known that Gene was even in that facility. . . . I expressed a silent prayer of thanks to Heavenly Father for His guiding influence which prompted my visit to St. Joseph Villa and led me to my dear friend."[18]

WHAT HAPPENS WHEN WE DON'T LISTEN TO PROMPTINGS

The stories you have read up to this point contain many great examples of men, women, and even children who listened to promptings from the Holy Ghost. I would like to conclude with a bad example, a very personal and gut-wrenching experience when I did not listen to the voice of the Spirit. It is my hope that you will learn from my mistake. I am very blessed that Heavenly Father gave me a second chance to be obedient to His promptings. Some may say, if you didn't listen to the prompting, why are you counting it as one of the 100 miracles in this book? Two reasons—first, although I was not obedient to the voice of the Spirit, it was still a miracle that the Holy Ghost warned me at all; and second, it was a miracle that my wife lived through the accident, as you will shortly see.

16 *You're Too Tired to Drive!*

Vickie's brother was married in the Mesa, Arizona temple in April 1979. It was a beautiful ceremony; the luncheon afterwards was excellent, and the reception later that evening went well.

18. Thomas S. Monson, "Peace, Be Still," *Ensign*, Nov. 2002, 53.

It was Saturday night, and we were tired after a very long day. Vickie's parents tried to convince us to spend the night and drive home on Sunday. We were anxious to get back to Provo though, as we were supposed to move out of our apartment on Monday and into a new place. We reasoned that if we traded off driving through the night, we could be back in Provo in time for Church Sunday afternoon.

We left Mesa about 10:00 p.m. It was about 2:00 a.m. when we stopped for gas in Kingman, Arizona. Although it has been over forty years, I can still remember the impression I had as I pulled into that gas station. I heard a voice—nothing audible—but a voice in my mind: "Jon, you're too tired to drive. Pull over and sleep."

I got out of the car to pump the gas and mulled over the impression. "No," I thought to myself, "We can do it. Vickie can sleep while I drive, and then I'll sleep while she drives. We're young; we can do it."

As I drove out of the gas station, I can still picture the exact location of the car when the impression came a second time, this time stronger: "Jon, you're too tired to drive!"

I considered the prompting a little longer; but if we stopped and slept, we wouldn't make it home in time for church. "No," I consciously said to myself. "We can do it."

By the time we hit Las Vegas, it was dawn, and we were dead tired. Vickie and I were now trading off driving at least every hour, yet we continued on.

When we got to Beaver, Utah, I pulled the car over and wearily said to Vickie, "It's your turn. I can't stay awake any longer." I had probably only been driving about thirty minutes. I crawled into the back seat where our baby Amber was sleeping. Vickie got behind the wheel. Next to her was our newly adopted son Jonathan. None of us were wearing seat belts; the importance of child seats and safety belts had only begun to be emphasized.

About twenty minutes later, I heard Vickie scream, "Jon, we're going off the road!"

I groggily looked up to see our little Pinto station wagon already in the large grass-covered median that separated the north and southbound lanes of Interstate 15. Witnesses later told me that when Vickie fell asleep at the wheel, she drifted from the far-right lane into the left lane and then off into the median.

I tried to keep her calm by saying, "It's all right, Vickie. Just gently put your foot on the brake and carefully slow down," but I couldn't get the words out in time. The car was out of control and had already gone onto the opposite side of the freeway.

In horror, we both saw vehicles now coming straight for us. Vickie quickly jerked the wheel to her right, and the car began to roll. Witnesses told us that the car rolled four times, into the median, and then back to the opposite side of the freeway.

I had always heard that shortly before a person thinks he's going to die, his entire life flashes before his eyes. It's true! In a matter of seconds, I saw everything I had ever done—good or bad—and I thought to myself, "I'm not ready to die."

When the car came to rest between the southbound lanes of the freeway, my first recollection was hearing our baby scream. I picked Amber up from the floor of the back seat and saw that she was fine, and then looked up to see that every window in our car was gone. I also saw something else that frightened me even more than what I had just experienced the past few seconds—Vickie was not in the driver's seat! I then realized that Jonathan wasn't in the front seat either.

I screamed out, "Vickie, where are you? Oh, Vickie, please be OK!"

I set Amber on the back seat and tried to open my door. It would not budge, so I scrambled into the front passenger seat and kicked the door open. The first thing I saw was Jonathan, about fifty feet from the car, running towards me. Blood was streaming down his face. He had obviously been thrown from the car but was well enough to run. But where was Vickie?

I looked to my right. There she was face down on the pavement only inches from the back of the car. Witnesses later told us that she had been thrown through the windshield onto the pavement, and then the car had landed right next to her—only inches away. I always marveled that the car had not landed on top of her.

"Oh Vickie," I cried as I ran to her and turned her body over. Her eyes were open, but glazed over. There was no response. I thought she was dead.

By this time, the horrified witnesses from several vehicles on both sides of the highway had stopped and come to our aid. One of them persuaded me not to move Vickie anymore and began first aid; another grabbed Jonathan and administered first aid to him. Still another kind stranger found the baby and took her to their car to calm and comfort her. A trucker got on his CB radio and called for an ambulance.[19]

It seemed like an eternity for the ambulance to come the twenty miles from Beaver, Utah. While we were waiting, Vickie came to consciousness. She looked up at me and said, "What happened?" She had no recollection of the accident—and never did.

With tears in my eyes, I gently told her, "Sweetheart, we've been in an accident."

There was a moment of silence, and then a startled look came to her scarred face. "I was driving, wasn't I?"

"Yes," I said.

She then began to sob, more like a pitiful moan. She cried out, "It's all my fault! It's all my fault!"

I knew it wasn't her fault. I remembered the still, small voice that had spoken to me several hours before and told me that we needed to pull over and sleep.

Vickie spent a week in the hospital recovering from the bruises and contusions she received from head to foot. Miraculously, not one bone in her body was broken. She always felt there were angels at the scene of the accident placing pillows at just the right places.

19. Although it has been forty years since the accident, tears are welling up in my eyes as I write about the kind strangers who stopped to help us. I never found out the names of those who helped us, but I can never forget their compassion and kindness.

Later in the week as Vickie recovered, I went to the wrecking yard where our car had been towed to retrieve what was salvageable of our possessions. I took one look at that mangled piece of metal and wondered how anyone could have survived. I was absolutely convinced that there was a reason why we were spared. This was no coincidence.

When I arrived home, there was a letter in the mailbox for me. It was from The Church of Jesus Christ of Latter-day Saints. My dream for several years had been to become a full-time seminary teacher for the Church. I had taken all the requisite classes and had student-taught a few months earlier. I held my breath as I opened the letter; I had been hired by the Church Educational System to teach seminary the coming fall.

Was that why we were spared? Was the Lord giving me a second chance? I now know the absolute importance of listening to the Spirit, and I have taught that principle hundreds of times since to thousands of Seminary and Institute students in Arizona, Colorado, Utah, and Wyoming.

IMPRESSIONS ON THE SOUL

President Joseph Fielding Smith said, "The impressions on the soul that come from the Holy Ghost are far more significant than a vision. It is where Spirit speaks to spirit, and the imprint upon the soul is far more difficult to erase."[20]

Since my blunder nearly forty years ago, I have come to appreciate what President Smith taught. I am a witness that one can learn to recognize and heed the quiet whisperings of the Spirit.

For those who are members of the Lord's church, after your baptism you were commanded to receive the gift of the Holy Ghost. To those who do, I promise it will always lead you right.[21]

---

20. Joseph Fielding Smith, *Seek Ye Diligently* (Salt Lake City: Deseret Book, 1970), 213.
21. Joseph Smith said, "If you will listen to the first promptings, you will get it right nine times out of ten." See Truman G. Madsen, *Joseph Smith the Prophet* (Salt Lake City: Bookcraft, 1989), 103.

Chapter 3

Answers to Prayer

"Be thou humble; and the Lord thy God shall lead thee by the hand, and give thee answer to thy prayers."
Doctrine and Covenants 112:10

---

17 *There Is a Key under That Rock*

The key didn't work. The Brown family had traveled all the way to Island Park, Idaho for a family vacation in a cabin loaned to them by friends, and the key they had been given didn't work.

The family spread out and walked around the house looking for open windows or other doors. Suddenly, they heard their seven-year-old son Steven shout that he had unlocked the front door.

Steven, with a big grin on his face, stood proudly inside the front doorway. When his father asked him how he had done it, Steven replied, "I bowed my head and prayed. When I looked up, my eyes spotted this big rock by the front steps, and I thought, 'There is a key under that rock.' And sure enough there it was."[1]

---

1. L. Edward Brown, "Pray unto the Father in My Name," *Ensign*, May 1997.

OUR RELATIONSHIP WITH GOD

Obviously, his parents had taught Steven the value of prayer. When the Lord taught Nephi to build a boat to cross to the Promised Land, he noted, "I did pray oft unto the Lord; wherefore the Lord showed unto me great things" (1 Nephi 18:3). What could be greater than answering a seven-year-old's prayer?

Heavenly Father wants to answer our prayers. How many times in scriptures does it say, "Ask . . . Seek . . . Knock?" The answer is *nine*!

One other observation about Steven—he obviously understood his relationship to God. I wonder how many times Steven had sung, "I am a Child of God" at Primary or at home? "As soon as we learn the true relationship in which we stand toward God (namely, God is our Father, and we are His children), then at once prayer becomes natural and instinctive on our part."[2]

As a father of six, I always wanted what was best for my children. I didn't always give them everything they asked for, but I always tried to give them what they needed. "Prayer is the act by which the will of the Father and the will of the children are brought into correspondence with each other. The object of prayer is not to change the will of God but to secure for ourselves and for others blessings that God is already willing to grant but that are made conditional on our asking for them."[3]

18 *Please Send Us Something Better*

Nobody in this dispensation knew better than Joseph Smith that God answers prayers. When he walked out of the sacred grove in upstate New York, he knew that God was real, and that he "would know to his latest breath" that God had answered a simple boy's prayer.[4]

Sometimes Joseph's prayers were answered in unusual ways. One mealtime, Emma had just served Johnnycake for dinner—again. It was a common meal for the poor on the American frontier. Johnnycake is a type of corn bread cooked

2. Bible Dictionary, "Prayer," 753.
3. Ibid.
4. Joseph Smith—History 1:24.

in a cast iron skillet. It kept starvation away if that was all you had to eat.

Emma called the family to dinner. Joseph looked at the Johnnycake and prayed, "Lord, we thank Thee for this Johnnycake, and ask Thee to send us something better. Amen."

Joseph cut the bread and passed a piece to each person. They heard a knock at the door.

"Is the Prophet Joseph at home?"

"I am," Joseph called out.

"I have brought you some flour and a ham."

Joseph rose from the table, took his gift, and blessed their visitor in the name of the Lord. When the man left, Joseph turned to Emma and said, "I knew the Lord would answer my prayer."[5]

EFFECTUAL AND FERVENT PRAYERS

My favorite scripture about prayer comes from James, the brother of Jesus: "The effectual fervent prayer of a righteous man availeth much" (James 5:16). "Effectual" is a fancy way of saying "effective." How often do you feel your prayers are effective? Have you pondered how you could give more effective prayers?

The word fervent comes from an old Latin word for "boiling." It literally means, "to glow." Do your prayers glow? Do your prayers feel sincere?

See if the following stories help you understand what James tried to teach—"The effectual fervent prayer of a righteous man availeth much."

19 *Your Prayers Have Been Heard*

They couldn't believe that their son wanted to come home from his mission. He had just arrived. What could they do to make him change his mind? They prayed for help.

That weekend, their stake conference featured Elder Thomas S. Monson, one of the youngest and newest members

5. John Lyman Smith, "Recollections of the Prophet Joseph Smith," *The Juvenile Instructor*, Mar. 15, 1892, 172.

of the Quorum of the Twelve Apostles. The couple requested a brief meeting with him.

Elder Monson met with the couple after conference in a quiet place, and they knelt in prayer. As Elder Monson prayed, the parents cried.

When they arose, the grieving father said, "Brother Monson, do you really think our Heavenly Father can alter our son's announced decision to return home before completing his mission? Why is it that now, when I am trying so hard to do what is right, my prayers are not heard?'

Elder Monson asked, "Where is your son serving?"

He replied, "Düsseldorf, Germany."

Elder Monson put his arms around them and said, "Your prayers have been heard and are already being answered. With more than twenty-eight stake conferences being held this day attended by the General Authorities, I was assigned to your stake. Of all the Brethren, I am the only one who has the assignment to meet with the missionaries in the Düsseldorf Germany Mission this very Thursday."

He did meet with the missionary who remained and completed his mission.[6]

20 *The Lord Has Sent Us*

Lonely and depressed, Ms. Annalore had contemplated suicide. What purpose was there in living? She knelt in prayer and cried out in anguish to God. She had already decided if she got no answer to her prayer, if he didn't show her some reason and purpose for living, she would take her life. Couldn't God give her some indication that He heard her prayer?

A knock came at her door twenty minutes later. Two missionaries from The Church of Jesus Christ of Latter-day Saints stood on her doorstep. They noticed something in her countenance, and the Spirit whispered to them to say something different in their door approach.

6. Thomas E. Monson, "The Prayer of Faith," *Ensign*, May 1978, 20.

"The Lord has sent us to tell you why you're here on earth."

Stunned, Ms. Annalore had just heard the very words of her prayer repeated in American accents. She invited the elders in and received all they taught to her as a direct message from God. It was as if she had always known these truths but had misplaced them momentarily. Instantly transformed, Sister Annalore was baptized the following week.[7]

PRAYER OF FAITH

Nine times in scripture the phrase "prayer of faith" is mentioned. One example: "And it is my will that you shall humble yourselves before me, and obtain this blessing by your diligence and humility and the *prayer of faith*" (Doctrine and Covenants 104:79, emphasis added).

As in all miracles, faith is essential. Why would you even bother to pray if you didn't believe someone was hearing you? When I pick up a telephone and dial 911 in an emergency, I *expect* someone to answer and give me help. How often when we pray do we really expect our Heavenly Father to be there and answer our cries for help?

Here is a wonderful story of a large group of Latter-day Saint youth who expected God to answer their prayer of faith followed by the story of a young woman who did not expect a miracle but was humbled by another young woman who did.

21 *Deliver Him Here*

For six months, the Latter-day Saint youth of New Zealand had prepared to sing and dance for the prophet of the Lord. President Spencer W. Kimball came to New Zealand for an area conference, and a cultural celebration had been planned the night before in a large college stadium.

Unfortunately, President Kimball became ill and ran a high fever. Camilla, his wife, who had accompanied him, was also sick. They would not be able to attend the cultural celebration and possibly not even the conference. President and

7. Richard H. Cracroft, "'We'll Sing and We'll Shout:' A Mantic Celebration of the Holy Spirit," Brigham Young University devotional, June 29, 1993, speeches.byu.edu.

Sister Kimball rested at the home of the New Zealand temple president while his first counselor N. Eldon Tanner presided at the cultural celebration.

As President Kimball slept, he was watched over by his doctor, Russell M. Nelson, who had recently been called as the General Sunday School President of the Church. Suddenly, President Kimball awoke.

"Brother Nelson, what time was that program to begin this evening?"

"At seven o'clock, President Kimball."

"What time is it now?"

"It's almost seven," Dr. Nelson replied.

"Tell Sister Kimball we're going."

Dr. Nelson checked President Kimball's temperature. It was normal. He took Sister Kimball's temperature. It was also normal.

Meanwhile at the college stadium, President Tanner began the cultural celebration by announcing that President and Sister Kimball were ill and would not be able to attend the evening festivities. He called on one of the New Zealand young men to pray. He prayed with great faith: "We are three-thousand New Zealand youth. We are assembled here, having prepared for six months to sing and dance for thy prophet. Wilt Thou heal him and deliver him here."

When the young man said "amen," and the thousands who had gathered unitedly echoed their approval, they opened their eyes. At that very moment, the car carrying President and Sister Kimball entered the stadium. A spontaneous shout of joy erupted throughout the stadium.[8]

8. Spencer J. Condie, *Russell M. Nelson: Father, Surgeon, Apostle* (Salt Lake City: Deseret Book, 2003), 172–74.

22 *His Pair of Glasses Rested in My Hands*

Beatrice and several of her Latter-day Saint friends had spent the day at a beach in southern France. Just before they were to return for the ninety-minute drive home, one of the men decided to take one more swim in the ocean. He forgot he was wearing his glasses and didn't take them off before diving in. They were gone.

The group needed to find his glasses, or they would all be stranded. He was the driver. Someone suggested they pray.

Beatrice, a recent convert, thought to herself, "Praying would avail us absolutely nothing." There was no way they could find those glasses in that huge ocean with waves continually rushing back and forth; besides, she felt uncomfortable with the idea of praying in public. Nevertheless, she bowed her head in the group prayer while they all stood "waist-deep in the murky water."

When the prayer ended, Beatrice stretched her arms back in the water to splash the group. She felt something—

"[H]is pair of glasses rested in my hand. A powerful feeling pierced my soul that God does actually hear and answer our prayers."[9]

STEP INTO THE DARKNESS

One of my favorite movie scenes comes from *Indiana Jones and the Last Crusade*. While in search for the Holy Grail, Indiana came to a huge chasm which he had to cross; he saw no possible way. With time running out, he finally decided to take "a leap of faith." He closed his eyes and took one giant step forward, half-expecting to fall to his death. Relieved when he did not fall, he found he had stepped onto a camouflaged bridge spanning the gulf.

Sometimes as we pray in faith, we are required, like Indiana Jones, to take a leap of faith. President Harold B. Lee said it another way

9. Neil L. Andersen, "Spiritually Defining Memories," *Ensign*, May 2020, 20.

when he taught us, "Walk to the edge of the light, and perhaps a few steps into the darkness, and you will find that the light will appear and move ahead of you."[10]

The Lord expects us to act upon our faith. There is a humorous anecdote about two boys walking home one day and deciding to take a shortcut through a farmer's field. The property clearly had a "No Trespassing" sign posted because of a large, surly bull. However, they couldn't see the bull, so they decided to take the risk. About halfway across the pasture—at the point of no return—the bull spotted them and charged in their direction. The boys began running, but one of them stopped and said, "Wait, let's kneel down and pray for help." The other boy said, "If you want to stop and kneel down and pray, you do it, but I'm going to *run and pray*."

That is good advice for everyone. President Dieter F. Uchtdorf said, "Often, the answer to our prayer does not come while we're on our knees but while we're on our feet serving the Lord and serving those around us."[11]

23 *The Contact Lens*

Elder Richard Cracroft had had his new contact lenses for only five days when disaster struck. He and his missionary companion were walking along a gravel road when a speck of dust flew into his right eye. He quickly removed the lens, cleaned it, and prepared to put it back in his eye. He placed it on his finger and was moving it towards his eye when a sudden gust of wind blew the contact away. Instead of 20/20 vision, Elder Cracroft now had 20/600—virtually blind in one eye.

He and his companion got down on their knees in a desperate search for the contact lens. For twenty minutes, they crawled around on the ground in vain. Elder Cracroft suggested they pray. Already on their knees, he pleaded for the Lord's help. Elder Cracroft reasoned with the Lord of his need

10. Harold B. Lee, Quoted by Boyd K. Packer, *The Holy Temple* (Salt Lake City: Bookcraft, 1980), 184.
11. Dieter F. Uchtdorf, "Waiting on the Road to Damascus," *Ensign*, May 2011, 76.

to see and of the appointments they had scheduled with interested investigators.

As they concluded the prayer and stood up, Elder Cracroft had a prompting. Without hesitation, he removed his remaining contact lens from his left eye. Blind in both eyes now, the step into the darkness had begun.

He told his companion to carefully watch where his second contact lens went. He stood in the exact place and position where he had lost the right lens. Placing the left lens on his finger, he moved it towards his face as before. Again, the wind blew the contact lens from his finger. He was now completely in the dark.

His companion said, "I see it. It's still in the air."

"Don't lose it," Elder Cracroft pled.

"It's still up," he whispered, now ten feet away. Then, from even further away, he exclaimed, "It's starting to fall."

"Keep your eye on it."

"I see it! I see it!" he said. There was a long pause and then, "Oh my gosh! Oh my gosh!"

Elder Cracroft waited. "Oh my gosh," he said, "it's landed, and"—pause— "it's landed almost right on top of the other lens!"

"You see the other lens?" he shouted.

"Yes, it's right here!"

Unable to see a thing, Elder Cracroft crawled over to him. Slowly, his companion placed both lenses in the palm of his hand.

The two missionaries again knelt in prayer, expressing their gratitude for the Lord's tender mercies.[12]

---

12. Richard H. Cracroft, "Divine Designs: Tracing the Lord's 'Pattern in All Things,'" Brigham Young University devotional, Dec. 10, 1996, speeches.byu.edu.

24 *I've Been Waiting for You*

Let me tell you one more personal experience from my mission to Vancouver, British Columbia, Canada. About a year in, I was serving in the mission home. When we weren't working in the office, we proselyted a large area of Vancouver, a city of over one million people. Because we worked at the mission offices during the day, evening was our only time to schedule appointments. Our proselyting time was precious.

On one particular night, we scheduled teaching appointments for 6:30, 7:30, and 8:30 p.m. Mission rules stated we were to leave our proselyting area by 9:30 and be home by 10:00 p.m.

Everything went according to plan until 8:30 p.m.—our appointment wasn't home. Now what do we do? Go tracting from door to door? Not a good idea so late at night in a big city—too many weird characters out there. Should we just go home early? No, that would waste a good hour of our valuable proselyting time. We could not think of anyone else to visit that late at night.

We stopped our vehicle by the side of the road and decided to ask for help. "Dear Heavenly Father," my companion prayed, "Please help us find someone who is ready to hear the gospel." When he finished the prayer, we sat quietly trying to listen for the still, small voice. Surely there must be someone in the city of Vancouver who was prepared to hear the gospel of Jesus Christ.

Suddenly I had an impression. I told my companion to turn the car around. He drove about two blocks before I told him to stop. The streets were dark, only lighted occasionally by a street lamp. We got out and walked up the rickety stairs of an old, two-story house. I knocked and anxiously waited.

An elderly woman answered the door. "Come in," she said, "I've been waiting for you."

Now you have to understand, that for most missionaries of The Church of Jesus Christ of Latter-day Saints, this almost never happens. The typical response is, "I'm not interested," or "I have my own religion," or "If you ever come back here again, I'll sic my dog on you." Many times, they'll look out the window and not even answer the door.

So, for someone to say, "Come in; I've been waiting for you," before we even had the chance to say hello and give our standard door approach was extremely unusual. It had never happened to me before.

I said, "Do you even know who we are?"

"You're the Mormon missionaries. Come in; I've been expecting you."

We entered her living room and sat down on a couch across from the woman. She then explained, "Two weeks ago, I met a member of your Church from across town. We had an interesting conversation about the Mormon religion. He said he was going to send some missionaries to talk with me. I'm glad you finally came. I've been wondering why it took him so long to send you."

Neither my companion nor I had received any phone call, letter, or any other message from anyone about this woman's interest in the gospel. Well, we did get the message but not from any earthly source. Was it just a coincidence or truly an answer to prayer? I had no doubt.

25 *Stop the Boys on the Bike*

Jerry had been a Protestant his entire life. Both of his parents had been ministers, so he had a deep belief in God. One day a friend shared with him that she had been contemplating suicide. She was depressed over the death of a child, a bitter divorce, and her struggles to be the single parent of four children.

Jerry didn't know exactly what to say, but he lovingly expressed that there was a purpose in life. He invited her to come to his church; she said she had given up on God. He wasn't sure what else he could do. He went outside to water his trees and silently prayed for guidance.

As he prayed, he heard a voice in his mind saying, "Stop the boys on the bikes."

What did that mean? Stop the boys on the bikes? As he pondered, he looked up the street and saw two boys on bikes.

Two young men in white shirts and ties were riding bicycles directly toward him. Stunned by what he thought was a coincidence, he watched them ride by. Suddenly, he realized he should do something. "Hey, you, please stop! I need to talk to you!"

The boys on the bikes approached Jerry. He noticed they wore name tags that said, "The Church of Jesus Christ of Latter-day Saints;" they were obviously missionaries.

Jerry looked at them and said, "This may sound a little weird, but I was praying and was told to 'stop the boys on the bikes.' I looked up the street, and here you are. Can you help me?"

The missionaries smiled, "Yes, I am sure we can."

Soon the missionaries were meeting with Priscilla, her children, and Jerry. As they learned about the plan of salvation, Priscilla began to have hope, and Jerry's already strong faith in Jesus Christ grew stronger. They were all soon baptized and became members of the Lord's church.[13]

PRAY WITHOUT CEASING

As the first of God's children on this earth, Adam and Eve were told to "call upon God in the name of the Son forevermore" (Moses 5:8).

In our dispensation, the Lord renewed the commandment to pray through a revelation to the Prophet Joseph Smith: "And again, I command thee that thou shalt pray vocally as well as in thy heart; yea, before the world as well as in secret, in public as well as in private" (Doctrine and Covenants 19:28).

I hope, however, that none of us prays to our Father in Heaven *because* it is a commandment. Hopefully, we talk to our earthly father and mother because we *want* to, and not because it is a chore. To repeat what was said at the beginning of this chapter, "as soon as we

13. Russell M. Nelson, "Ask the Missionaries! They Can Help You!" *Ensign*, Nov. 2012, 19–20.

learn the true relationship in which we stand toward God, then at once prayer becomes natural and instinctive on our part."[14]

One concluding thought: the apostle Paul wrote to the Thessalonians that they should "pray without ceasing" (1 Thessalonians 5:17). The word "ceasing" caught my attention recently because I have been writing this book based around the idea, "Has the day of miracles ceased?" I believe that, as long as there is one person on the face of this earth who sincerely and fervently prays without ceasing, miracles will not end

14. Bible Dictionary, "Prayer," 753.

Chapter 4

Fasting and Prayer

"[T]his kind goeth not out but by prayer and fasting."
Matthew 17:21

26 *He Would Need Both of His Eyes*

Dan's father gave him some matches to start the campfire. His family had stopped to camp for the night, on their way to southern Montana for a reunion. As Dan scraped his match on a rock, a flame ignited but at the same time, the match head broke off and flew into his eye. He screamed in terrible pain.

Dan's mother got some ice from the cooler to help stop the burning pain. After a few minutes, his parents were able to get Dan to open his eye to assess the damage. It didn't look good; his normally brown eye was now completely white.

They headed to the nearest hospital located in Helena, Montana. The eye specialist gave terrible news to the family—Dan was now blind in one eye. He was given some medicine for infection, an eye patch, and told to come back in a few days.

The entire family decided to hold a twenty-four-hour fast for Dan's full recovery. At the end of their fast, his father gave Dan a priesthood blessing. His sister observed, "My dad told Dan that the Lord loved him and had many things for him to do in this life. He also told him he would need both of his eyes to complete his mission on earth, that his eye would heal, and that his vision would be fully restored."

The next day when the doctor in Helena removed Dan's eye patch and looked into his eye, he said to his parents, "Are you sure this eye was the injured one? This eye is perfectly normal."

The confused doctor checked the other eye that was also normal. "It is impossible for an eye to heal like that," he said. "I have no explanation for it."

Dan's family had an explanation for it: through fasting, prayer, faith, and the power of God's holy priesthood, Dan was healed. A miracle had occurred.[1]

FASTING: A PRINCIPLE OF POWER

Sometimes prayer is not enough. Sometimes our spirits need a little boost.

Have you ever been part of a booster club? Booster clubs serve as sources of help and encouragement to schools, athletic teams, or various other school activities. They seek to increase and improve the power and effectiveness of the sponsoring group. Without booster clubs, many organizations would never be able to succeed.

Fasting combined with prayer increases our faith and power, like our own personal booster club. Who supports us better than the Father, the Son, and the Holy Ghost? I couldn't think of a better booster club than that!

In a New Testament account, Jesus came upon a group of His disciples who had been unable to heal a man whose young son was possessed by a devil. He asked to see the boy and said to the father, "If thou canst believe, all things are possible to him that believeth."

The father "cried out, and said with tears, Lord, I believe; help thou mine unbelief" (Mark 9:23–24).

This man, whose faith was weak from dealing with a child beset with difficult problems his entire life, needed a boost. Jesus provided it, and the boy was healed.

Later, when the crowds had left, and they were alone, the apostles asked Jesus why they had been unable to perform the miracle.

---

1. Debra J. Workman, "Believing is Seeing," *New Era*, March 2005, 24.

Jesus replied, "This kind goeth not out but by prayer *and* fasting" (Matthew 17:21, emphasis added).

Prayer, in and of itself, is a powerful tool. When combined with fasting, the two become synergistic.

I had a friend who taught me about synergy when he showed me his new tandem bicycle—a fancy bicycle-built for two. "Synergy," he told me, "is when 1 + 1 = 3."

"What?" I said with a confused look.

"It's when two elements, combined together, create an effect that is greater than the sum of each individual part." He went on to explain that two people on a tandem bicycle could actually produce more energy together than working alone: 1 + 1 = 3.

Why is fasting combined with prayer so powerful and synergistic? Before discussing that, read the next miracle.

27 *Now I'm Ready*

"Bishop, hurry up to the hospital and give my child a blessing." Her son lay in a Honolulu hospital extremely sick with polio. Polio is a potent virus that can cause paralysis, severe disabilities, and even death.

The bishop, an independently wealthy businessman, received the desperate phone call one morning. He did not go to the hospital at all that day. In fact, it wasn't until the next afternoon that he arrived at the hospital.

The irate mother lashed out at him, "You, my bishop, your own boss. I asked you to come and bless my child seriously ill, and you didn't show up."

The bishop waited patiently for her to unload her frustrations and then said, "When I hung up the receiver yesterday, I started to fast. I've been fasting and praying. Now I'm ready."

By the power of the Melchizedek priesthood, and in the spirit of fasting and prayer, he blessed the child.

The boy went home that evening.[2]

2. Matthew Cowley, "Miracles," Brigham Young University devotional, Feb. 18, 1953, speeches.byu.edu.

FASTING COMBINED WITH PRAYER

Couldn't the bishop have simply knelt in prayer and gone to the hospital? What did he gain by adding fasting to his prayers?

Let me suggest a few things that are gained when fasting is combined with prayer?

- Confidence
- Increased Faith
- Humility
- Clarity (knowing the will of the Lord)
- Spiritual Power
- Focus

These qualities promote miracles. Additionally, fasting and prayer help us provide for the poor and needy, fortify ourselves against temptation, increase our spirituality, broaden our shoulders for times of adversity, and open the windows of heaven.

Hopefully, the following latter-day miracles connected with fasting and prayer will strengthen your testimony of these principles.

28 *The God of Heaven Has Done This for You*

Members of The Church of Jesus Christ of Latter-day Saints now live in 196 nations and territories.[3] All countries tell their own stories of the miracles it took to allow the Church of Jesus Christ to be established there. I am sure that fasting and prayer were involved in almost every one. The following example took place in Italy.

Elder Lorenzo Snow was called as a young man to open Italy for the preaching of the gospel. He wasn't having success—not one person had been converted.

He and his companion had felt impressed to labor in a small village nestled among the beautiful Alps in the northern

3. Church statistics as of September 3, 2020, see Gerrit W. Gong, "All Nations, Kindreds, and Tongues," *Ensign*, Nov. 2020, 39.

part of Italy. They made friends with a family who had a critically ill child.

Elder Snow had an impression that if this boy were healed, the miracle would soften the hearts of the people in that village and, eventually, the nation.

He and his companion began to fast and pray. They climbed to a place of seclusion above the village. For six hours they pled with the Lord to allow them to use the divine power of the priesthood to restore that little boy's health.

The reply came, "Yes."

With perfect faith brought through fasting and prayer, the missionaries walked down the mountain and blessed the dying child. He was promised that he would live.

When they checked back with the family a few hours later, they found the boy already improving and well on his way to a full recovery.

As a parent of six children myself, I can only imagine the gratitude those parents had towards two humble missionaries. Elder Snow told the parents, "The God of heaven has done this for you."[4]

The baptisms soon came, and the first branch of the Church in Italy was established.

29 *Will You Be Our Pastor?*

The gospel had been well established in England for seventy years when Elder Brown received his mission call to serve there. Early in the 20th century, missionaries sometimes served without companions. I can only imagine how frightening that would have been to me anytime during my mission, especially in the beginning.

He was sent to Norwich where the district president informed him that he was being sent to Cambridge. "I want you to go with Elder Downs. Elder Downs will leave the morning after you get there for France because his mission is completed."

4. Eliza R. Snow, *Biography and Family Record of Lorenzo Snow* (Salt Lake City: Deseret News Company, 1884), 128–29.

I think right then I would have panicked. After one day as a missionary, he was alone. It gets better.

The district president continued, "You might be interested to know, Brother Brown, that the last Mormon elder that was in Cambridge was driven out by a mob at the point of a gun and was told that the next Mormon elder that stepped inside the city limits would be shot on sight. I thought you would be glad to know that."

I'm thinking, *Are you kidding me? When is the next boat for America?* That's what Elder Woodstock would have said. There's more.

When Elders Brown and Downs arrived in Cambridge, they saw anti-Mormon banners all over the city. The word had gotten out that the Mormons were coming.

Elder Downs helped his inexperienced companion by preparing some missionary pamphlets and writing his name and address on them. He showed Elder Brown where to start contacting people the next morning, and then he left for Paris.

For three days, Elder Brown went from door to door. Not one person would talk to him; and many doors were slammed in his face. He felt hopeless, forlorn, and alone; there was not another Latter-day Saint within 120 miles of Cambridge.

Saturday, after a morning with the same result, he came back to his flat for lunch and to warm himself by the fireplace. Someone knocked at the door. The landlady answered the door, and he heard a man say, "Is there an Elder Brown here?"

The man entered the room holding one of the missionary pamphlets. "Are you Elder Brown?" he said, surprised to see such a young man before him. "Did you leave this tract [pamphlet] under my door?"

Elder Brown couldn't deny it, "Yes, sir, I did." He waited for the worst to happen.

The visitor began, "Last Sunday there were seventeen of us heads of families who left the Church of England. We went to my home, where I have a rather large room. . . . We decided that we would pray all through the week that the Lord would send us a new pastor. When I came home tonight, I was discouraged; I thought our prayer had not been answered. But when I found this tract under my door, I knew the Lord had answered our prayer. Will you come tomorrow night and be our new pastor?"

Elder Brown had been a missionary for three days; he hadn't even attended a church meeting since arriving in England. He wasn't even sure what a pastor was, but he looked at the man and said, "Yes, I'll come."

At this point, I would have pulled out my cell phone and called my mission president for help. There were no phones available to Elder Brown, but he did have fasting and prayer.

He told his landlady he would not be eating and retired to his room to pray. He prayed to his Father in Heaven like he had never prayed before. "I told Him of my predicament. I pleaded for His help. I asked Him to guide me. I pleaded that He would take it off my hands."

When he didn't feel he was getting anywhere with his prayers, he got off his knees and went to bed. Sleep would not come. He fell back down on his knees and continued to pray all night long.

Elder Brown continued his fast the next morning; he spent most of the day walking around the campus of Cambridge University. He continued to pray throughout the day since his appointment was not until seven that evening.

The man he had met the day before met him at the door. He bowed very low and politely said, "Come in, Reverend, sir." That scared him to death.

As he entered the very large room, the entire congregation stood out of respect for their new pastor. He really got scared then because he had not even considered what he would do next. It had not occurred to him that he would have to do all the preaching and praying, and as it turned out, all the singing too.

He began, "Let's sing 'O My Father.'" The congregation looked at him with blank stares ("O My Father was written by the Latter-day Saint, Eliza R. Snow). He began to sing—a solo.

Shaking badly, and so they wouldn't be looking at him, he asked them to turn around and kneel down by your chairs while he prayed.

They knelt, and he prayed. Elder Brown later said, "And for the second time in my life, I talked with God. All fear left me. I didn't worry anymore. I was turning it over to Him." In part, he prayed, "Father in Heaven, these folks have left the Church of England. They have come here tonight to hear the truth. You know that I am not prepared to give them what they want, but Thou art, O God, the one who can. And if I can be an instrument through whom You speak, very well, but please take over."

Everyone arose from their knees after the prayer and turned around; most of them were in tears. Elder Brown wisely dispensed with another hymn and began preaching. He spoke for forty-five minutes. "I don't know what I said. I didn't talk—God spoke through me, as subsequent events proved."

When the meeting ended, the people crowded around him and kissed and held his hands. Elder Brown floated back to his apartment. Within three months, every man, woman, and child (over the age of eight) in that room had been baptized members of The Church of Jesus Christ of Latter-day Saints.

When Elder Brown shared that story at a Brigham Young University devotional more than 60 years later, he was now President Hugh B. Brown of the Quorum of the Twelve Apostles, first counselor in the First Presidency.[5]

30 *Bishop, Taina Has Cancer*

A cancer diagnosis is difficult, and the heartache can be especially painful when the diagnosis is for one of your own children.

Tongan Bishop Leni Tu'ihalangingie noticed one day that his oldest daughter, Taina, was walking strangely, one foot dragging behind the other. Her condition worsened during the next week even though she felt no pain.

5. Hugh B. Brown, "'Father, Are You There?'" Brigham Young University devotional, Oct. 8, 1967, speeches.byu.edu.

The medication the doctors prescribed did not help. Two months passed, and Taina's foot was now extremely painful; nothing brought relief.

She spent ten days in the local hospital undergoing tests. The tests had to be sent from Tonga to New Zealand for interpretation and diagnosis. Finally, the doctor announced the results to the anxious parents: "Bishop, Taina has bone cancer; we feel her leg should be amputated."

Before he would consent, Bishop Tu'ihalangingie asked to take his daughter home for a while. He began to fast and pray.

Forty-eight hours later he invited his two counselors and the high priest group leader to join him in administering to Taina. He blessed her and promised her that she would be completely healed.

He said, "Although my heart was extremely troubled, at the moment I pronounced the blessing, all troubled feelings and doubts were swept away. I knew Heavenly Father had heard my cry and honored my promises to Taina. It was a happy day in my life."

Two weeks later, Taina went back to the hospital for further testing. She walked normally again, and the tests showed no sign of cancer.

Taina later served a full-time mission in the Salt Lake City, Utah.[6]

OVERCOMING ADDICTIONS

When Jesus told His disciples, "This kind goeth not out save by prayer and fasting," he had just healed a boy possessed by a devil. The boy had become a slave to the evil spirit within him. When people are struggling with addictions of any kind, could it not be said about them that they have become slaves to that addiction?

The prophet Isaiah taught about the power of fasting. He said that one of the purposes of fasting was "to loose the bands of wickedness,

6. Eric B. Shumway, *Tongan Saints: Legacy of Faith* (Institute for Polynesian Studies, 1991), 262–63.

to undo the heavy burdens, and to let the oppressed go free, and that ye break every yoke" (Isaiah 58:6).

Is it possible that the same formula of fasting and prayer that Jesus spoke of in casting out devils could be applied to addictions? I believe the answer is an emphatic yes! Addictions are powerful and require every possible weapon available in our spiritual arsenal. As we sincerely and fervently approach the throne of heaven through fasting and prayer, we can obtain increased spiritual strength. We will then have the faith and confidence to call down the powers of heaven on our behalf.[7]

31 *I Have No Desire to Smoke*

The missionaries taught a man who really wanted to join the Church. He knew it was true but—he was addicted to tobacco. He had tried so many times to quit. The missionaries prayed for him, and with him. His wife, already a strong member of the Church, constantly prayed for him, but he felt like he was just too weak.

One night, the missionaries felt inspired to invite him to fast for help in overcoming his addiction. They told him that they would fast with him; his wife agreed to join in also.

Fasting in the Church is usually done in a twenty-four period; however, these two missionaries felt impressed to ask this man and his wife to fast for two days. They agreed, and the fast began.

Forty-eight hours later, they all met together and knelt in solemn prayer to implore Heavenly Father to help this man overcome his addiction. Each person took a turn praying. The prayers were all basically the same: please take the desire to smoke from this man.

The addicted smoker was the last to pray. When he finished, he stood up and announced, "I have no desire to smoke." He never smoked again. After baptism and receiving the gift of the Holy Ghost, he became a faithful member of

7. For a wonderful sermon on how fasting can give us the power to change our lives, see Elder Shayne M. Bowen, "Fasting with Power," *Ensign*, May 2009, 64–67.

the Church and served in numerous callings including in his ward bishopric and in the stake young men's presidency.[8]

"This kind goeth not out save by prayer and fasting."

THE FOUR Ps OF FASTING

I want to conclude this chapter with a little bit of advice about fasting that comes from a lot of experience. When I was younger, I looked upon fasting as a duty—almost like a necessary evil. I felt miserable going 24 hours without food and water. As you may deduce, those fasts were neither spiritual nor effective experiences.

As I grew older, I gradually started to look forward to fasting. The secret was in discovering the four Ps of fasting:

- Preparation
- Purpose
- Pondering
- Prayer

Preparation includes placing fasting on your calendar well in advance so you can mentally prepare for sacred experiences. For example, planning a party the night before fasting is never a good idea. Preparing in advance also gives you time to plan a good meal and to drink plenty of water before beginning the fast.

Part of that preparation includes thinking about why you want to fast. Fasting without a purpose is just going hungry, which is never fun. Fasting with a purpose gives true meaning to the act and sustains your spirit while your physical body is reacting to the lack of food and water.

Once you begin fasting, do a lot of pondering. Every time your stomach growls, ask yourself, "Why am I fasting?" Ponder in your mind your purpose for this particular fast; soon the hunger pangs diminish.

And of course, don't forget prayer. Almost every time fasting is mentioned in the scriptures, the word prayer accompanies it. As was mentioned earlier in the chapter, fasting and prayer are synergistic and become a powerful force for good.

8. Hartman Rector, Jr., in Conference Report, Apr. 1970, 140–41.

I testify that fasting and prayer are principles of the gospel of Jesus Christ for developing spiritual strength. They have helped me control my appetites and passions, have helped me resist temptations, and have given me spiritual insights to important questions and life-changing decisions. Fasting and prayer have given me strength in times of trial and blessed me throughout my life.

32 *It Was at Sunset*

Emily Stratton had been the Primary president in the Virgin Ward in southern Utah for fifteen years. One day, word swept through the small town that Sister Stratton had lost her eyesight following a sudden illness.

The local doctor sent her to the hospital in St. George for treatment. After several weeks, no treatments had been successful; she was totally blind.

The Primary children and teachers from her ward decided to hold a special fast. At sunset the next day, they met at the chapel to close their fast with prayer. They pleaded in Sister Stratton's behalf. They felt peace and knew that Heavenly Father had answered their prayers.

When Sister Stratton arrived home a few days later, the children gathered to meet her and tell of her of their special fast.

"What time was your fast meeting, children?" Sister Stratton asked.

"It was at sunset," one child exclaimed.

Sister Stratton's eyes filled with tears. "At sunset on that day, I was sitting in a chair by the west window of my hospital room. As I looked up, I saw the sunset for the first time since the fever stole my sight. Yes, children, I can see!"

Emily Stratton was blessed with perfect eyesight for the rest of her life.[9]

---

9. Diane K. Cahoon, "Sister Stratton's Miracle," *The Friend*, June 1997.

Chapter 5

Administration to the Sick

"They shall lay hands on the sick, and they shall recover."
Mark 16:18

---

33 *Come Back, and See What You Have Done for Me*

Two missionaries serving on the Navajo Indian Reservation walked into the simple hogan of a native woman. She lay on a sheepskin on the ground having been unable to walk for six long years. The missionaries visited with her for a few minutes and then started to leave.

She called them back and said, "Isn't there something you do for sick people?"

"Yes."

"Please do it for me."

Two humble missionaries dropped to their knees and administered to her by the authority of the priesthood and in the name of Jesus Christ.

The missionaries left the hogan. They had not gone far when they heard, "Come back and see what you have done for me." The elders turned around to see the woman they had just blessed standing on her feet and walking after them.[1]

HEALINGS BY THE LAYING ON OF HANDS

In the three previous chapters, I wrote of many miracles performed by those who listened to the promptings of the Holy Ghost, used the power of prayer, and the added power of fasting. This chapter illustrates an actual priesthood ordinance—the laying on of hands to administer to the sick by those who have proper authority.

Jesus did it: "Now when the sun was setting, all they that had any sick with divers diseases brought them unto him, and he laid his hands on every one of them, and healed them" (Luke 4:40). His disciples did it: "And it came to pass, that the father of Publius lay sick of a fever and of a bloody flux: to whom Paul entered in, and prayed, and laid his hands on him, and healed him" (Acts 28:8). Latter-day disciples are commanded to do it: "Lay your hands upon the sick, and they shall recover" (Doctrine and Covenants 66:9).

34 *I Rebuked the Pain in the Name of Christ*

Serving as a new missionary in rural Ohio, Elder Orson Whitney loved to testify to people that there were miracles in the Church of Jesus Christ today as in days of old. One day, "a sick woman took [him] at [his] word and sent for [him]."

Suddenly, Elder Whitney realized he had never given a priesthood blessing before. He feared that if she were not healed, he would be deemed an imposter.

The woman had suffered for six weeks with neuralgia—constant nerve pain. He laid his hands on her head and proceeded to bless her using the authority of the holy priesthood bestowed upon him.

"No sooner had I laid my hands upon the woman's head, than power came over me that I had never felt before," he

1. Matthew Cowley, "Miracles," Brigham Young University devotional, Feb. 18, 1953, speeches.byu.edu.

described. "It was a burning in my bosom, so powerful as to almost deprive me of speech, and it went like fire to the very tips of my fingers." He rebuked the woman's pain in the name of Jesus Christ. She was instantly healed.

"Thank God!" she said. "The pain has gone."

Overcome by the goodness and power of God, Elder Orson F. Whitney sank into a chair and burst into tears.[2]

PRIESTHOOD POWER

To obtain the priesthood is to obtain the authority to act in the name of God. To obtain *power* to exercise that priesthood is something different. Power comes through righteousness. "When I lay hands on the sick, I expect the healing power and influence of God to pass through me to the patient and the disease to give way," taught President Brigham Young. He went on to say where that power comes from: "When we are prepared, when we are holy vessels before the Lord, a stream of power from the Almighty can pass through the tabernacle of the administrator to the system of the patient, and the sick are made whole."[3]

To reiterate what I said in an earlier chapter, perfection is not needed to perform miracles—righteousness is. Righteousness is striving to keep the commandments such as paying your tithing, living the Word of Wisdom, and living the law of chastity. Think of a temple recommend interview. Your bishop does not expect perfection to qualify for a temple recommend, but he does expect high standards. If you have broken one of the commandments, he expects you to take the proper steps for complete repentance.

I illustrate this principle with a sacred personal experience. I know better than any person living that I am an imperfect man. I constantly make mistakes, but I also constantly repent. Most of the time, I feel worthy enough to partake of the sacrament every Sunday and participate in priesthood ordinances. Occasionally, miracles happen.

2. Orson F. Whitney, in Conference Report, Apr. 1925, 20. Elder Orson F. Whitney served as a member of the Quorum of Twelve from 1906–1931.
3. *Teachings of Presidents of the Church: Brigham Young* (Salt Lake City: The Church of Jesus Christ of Latter-day Saints, 1997), 252.

35 One Second Later, the Pain Left

My wife, Vickie, had begun to have gall bladder problems when in her early fifties. Sudden attacks became more and more frequent. She experienced excruciating and debilitating pain during these episodes. At first, the pain would last only a few minutes; eventually the pain grew stronger and lasted longer.

One night she awoke me out of a sound sleep and begged me to give her a blessing. She was having another gall bladder attack and was suffering from unbelievable pain and suffering. Tears were streaming down her face.

I got out of bed, walked around to her side, and laid my hands upon her head. By the authority of the holy Melchizedek Priesthood, I blessed her and told her that she would immediately begin to feel better.

I was later humbled to read in her journal: "One second later, the pain left. It felt like a soft caress starting from Jon's hands on my head and went down my body to my toes. As it went, it took all my pain away; within fifteen seconds, I was completely pain free. I was so happy. Even now as I recall the experience, I am filled with thanksgiving and gratitude. It really helped my testimony grow of the power of the priesthood and the love of the Lord."[4]

36 Aren't You an Elder?

Thomas S. Monson was just eighteen when he enlisted in the navy and was ordained an elder one week before reporting for active duty. Eighteen-year-olds are usually far from perfect, but he always tried to stay on the strait and narrow path.

A counselor in his ward bishopric met him at the train station and gave him the *Missionary Handbook.* Thomas laughed and commented, "I'm not going on a mission."

He answered, "Take it anyway. It may come in handy."

It did.

---

4. Personal journal of Vickie Church Woodstock, August 3, 2009.

In basic training, the commanding officer instructed the new recruits on the best way to pack their clothing in a large sea bag: "If you have a hard, rectangular object you can place in the bottom of the bag, your clothes will stay more firm." Thomas immediately thought of the *Missionary Handbook* and placed it at the bottom of his bag for twelve weeks.

Every soldier looked forward to Christmas leave when they would go home for the first time since arriving for basic training. Unfortunately, the night before they were to leave, Thomas's good friend, Leland Merrill, became extremely ill.

Listening to the moans coming from the next bunk, Thomas said, "What's the matter, Merrill?"

"I'm sick," he replied. "I'm really sick."

Thomas told him to go to the base dispensary (a hospital clinic for soldiers), but he knowingly answered that such a decision would prevent him from being home for Christmas.

Leland's moans grew throughout the night. Suddenly he whispered, "Monson, Monson, aren't you an elder?"

"Yes."

"Give me a blessing."

Thomas immediately implored his Heavenly Father for help. He had never given a priesthood blessing. He had never witnessed a priesthood blessing given. He had never even received a priesthood blessing. How was he supposed to know what to do?

As he silently prayed, he felt an impression: "Look in the bottom of the sea bag."

At two o'clock in the morning, Thomas dumped the contents of his bag on the floor, picked up *The Missionary Handbook,* and read how one blesses the sick. With about seventy curious sailors looking on, he administered to Leland. Before he could stow his gear, Leland Merrill was sleeping like a child.

The next morning, Leland smiled at his friend and said, "Monson, I'm glad you hold the priesthood."[5]

5. Thomas S. Monson, "The Army of the Lord," *Ensign,* May 1979, 37.

ANOINTING WITH OIL

Sometimes oil is used in administering to the sick. Consecrated oil has been used in priesthood ordinances for centuries. Moses was told to anoint his brother Aaron and his sons "and consecrate them, and sanctify them" (Exodus 28:41). The prophet Samuel anointed Saul and David (1 Samuel 10:1; 16:13).

When Jesus sent His twelve apostles forth to preach the gospel two by two, "they anointed with oil many that were sick, and healed them" (Mark 6:13).

James, a half-brother of Jesus and also an apostle, told the members of the Church, "Is any sick among you? let him call for the elders of the church; and let them pray over him, anointing with oil in the name of the Lord: and the prayer of faith shall save the sick, and the Lord shall raise him up" (James 5:14–15).

The oil used in administering to the sick is to be pure olive oil. We are not exactly sure why olive oil is to be used other than that the Lord has commanded it. We do know that oil pressed from olives was considered anciently as the purest and cleanest of oils. Joseph Fielding Smith wrote, "We find through all the prophetic writings that olive trees and olive oil are emblems of sacredness and purity."[6]

The oil is first consecrated by a priesthood holder and set apart specifically for the purpose of anointing the sick and the afflicted and not to be used for other purposes thereafter.

The use of oil in administering to the sick is not essential; priesthood blessings by the laying on of hands can be given without it.

When oil is used to administer to the sick, there are two components. First, a Melchizedek priesthood holder places a drop of oil on the crown of the person's head, or as near as possible if injury prevents. He then lays both of his hands on the recipient's head and, by the authority of the priesthood, anoints him or her. Like all priesthood ordinances, the anointing is concluded in the name of Jesus Christ.

The second component is called sealing the anointing. After the anointing, two or more Melchizedek priesthood holders then unitedly lay their hands on the person's head. One of them, acting as spokesman

6. Joseph Fielding Smith, Jr., *Answers to Gospel Questions*, 5 vols. (Salt Lake City: Deseret Book Co., 1957–66), 1:152.

then seals the anointing. "To seal something means to affirm it, to make it binding for its intended purpose," said President Dallin H. Oaks. "When elders anoint a sick person and seal the anointing, they open the windows of heaven for the Lord to pour forth the blessing He wills for the person afflicted."[7]

Let's look at three examples.

37 *He Has Been Run Over by a Car*

"Help!"

Phil was in his backyard when he heard his neighbor a few houses away screaming for help. Without hesitation, Phil ran at full speed down the block.

Ken held the youngest of his eight children in one of his arms; with the other, he held a container of consecrated oil.

Handing the oil to Phil, Ken said, "I want you to anoint my son. Quickly! He has been run over by a car!"

Phil was surprised by the calm in his friend's voice. There was a great deal of tension of course, but there was no panic even though the child gasped for air.

Phil took the oil and anointed the small boy. Then he, Ken, and another neighbor who also held the Melchizedek Priesthood together laid their hands on the child. Acting as voice, Ken sealed the anointing and commanded his son to live until he could reach the hospital and receive proper medical assistance.

When they opened their eyes, the baby was turning blue from lack of oxygen, but they felt calm. They felt the warmth of the Spirit quietly whisper that the baby would be okay.

The parents rushed their son to the hospital. Phil stayed with the rest of Ken's children. All they could do now was pray and wait.

After what seemed like an eternity, the phone rang. Phil answered as the anxious children listened in.

"Hello! Yes, Ken, this is Phil. How's the baby?"

7. Dallin H. Oaks, "Healing the Sick," *Ensign*, May 2010, 49.

Silence, then, "That's great," Phil sighed.

The children yelled and screamed for joy.

"Quiet!" Phil yelled, "There's more. Go ahead, Ken, I couldn't hear the last part."

When Phil hung up the telephone, he turned to the children. "Your little brother is okay," he said, "but they must keep him there for awhile to make sure nothing goes wrong. His lungs were crushed, and the doctors don't know how he even survived, but he'll be fine after a lot of good care."

The doctors were unable to explain the miracle, but they hadn't been present when Phil anointed the child with consecrated oil and his father had sealed the anointing and blessed him.[8]

38 *The Nuns Expected Someone to Administer the Last Rites*

A family of six drove home to Utah from the Eastern United States. Their car collided head-on with a semi-truck in Illinois. One boy was killed, another suffered a broken leg, and the mother was left in critical condition. The father and the remaining two children were only slightly injured.

The local bishop called two Melchizedek Priesthood holders to go to the hospital and give the mother, Sharon, a blessing. The doctors did not expect her to live; her skull was crushed, she had a broken arm, a deep cut over her eyes, and internal injuries as well. Since it was a Catholic hospital, the nuns expected someone to administer the last rites to her. Sharon had asked for a priesthood blessing instead.

Soon, two priesthood holders entered her hospital room. The doctors had given up hope, and left saying there was no hope for saving her life.

One of the priesthood holders searched Sharon's head for a spot to apply the consecrated oil, a difficult task because her

8. Robert Marcum, "Preparation for Power," *New Era*, May 1983, 48–50.

skull was so severely injured. He finally anointed her temple, as this was the only accessible place.

Both of the men then laid their hands on her head. The brother giving the blessing struggled to find the right words to say as he had never administered to someone who was dying. He later recalled, "I gave the Spirit full rein. I remember assuring her that she would live to raise her children, that her earthly mission was not yet over, that her family still needed her, and that her injuries would heal quickly."

The nuns were stunned at the words of the blessing. How could this woman live? One of the nuns spoke with the priesthood brethren after the blessing; she was excited to think that Sharon had a chance for recovery. The same nun called one of them the next day to say that Sharon wanted to see him.

She was sitting up in her hospital bed when he arrived, a bright smile on her face and a sparkle in her eyes. He noticed there was no sign of her skull injury, no evidence of bleeding or broken bone.

Two weeks later, Sharon walked out of the hospital with only her arm in a sling and a small bandage on her forehead.[9]

39 As a Doctor, I Doubted

Dr. James Mason was a prominent Latter-day Saint physician who at one time served as Assistant Secretary for Health, making him the head of the United States Public Health Service and Acting Surgeon General. He later served as a General Authority of The Church of Jesus Christ of Latter-day Saints.

As a young physician, Dr. Mason was called to the Primary Children's Medical Center in Salt Lake City one day to treat a nine-year-old boy. Three days earlier, the boy had complained of a headache and of not feeling well; he was running a fever. Over the next three days, he grew increasingly ill.

On the day he was brought to the hospital, he had lapsed into unconsciousness, and the family realized for the first time

9. Richard L. Emery, "They Expected Last Rites," *Ensign,* Feb. 1987, 40–41.

how seriously ill he was. After many tests and examinations, the boy was diagnosed with bacterial meningitis. When Dr. Mason left the boy's room, the child was unconscious with falling blood pressure; Mason had serious doubts the boy would survive.

His mother and father met the doctor in the hallway. "Doctor Mason, will you assist us in administering to our boy?"

The father anointed his small son with consecrated oil and asked the doctor to seal the anointing and pronounce the blessing. As they laid their hands on the critically ill child, the Spirit whispered to Dr. Mason, "Promise him he will recover. Promise him he'll have no aftereffects from this infection." In the name of Jesus Christ and by the power of the holy Melchizedek Priesthood, the blessing and promises were given.

As Dr. Mason left the room for the second time that evening, he had an assurance much stronger than that of medical science that the boy would live, and indeed he did. His recovery was complete.[10]

THE ROLE OF PRAYER IN PRIESTHOOD BLESSINGS

Priesthood blessings are not prayers; they are ordinances the priesthood holder acts in the name of God, doing what Jesus would do if He were present.

That is not to say that prayer should not accompany the administration. I was taught this lesson many years ago as a young Melchizedek priesthood holder.

Dave Kirkpatrick called me one evening and asked me to come to his home to assist him in giving his daughter a blessing. I immediately went, sat down, and chatted with the family for a few minutes to ascertain what was wrong. I then stood up, ready to get the blessing over with so I could go back home.

Dave said, "Wait a minute. Can we have a word of prayer first?"

I sat back down, and then Dave, sensing that I needed to be taught a valuable lesson, shared two verses from the Book of Mormon. "Ye shall

---

10. James O. Mason, "As a Doctor, I Doubted," *Ensign,* Aug. 1977, 58.

call on the Father in my name, in mighty prayer; and *after* ye have done this ye shall have power that to him upon whom ye shall lay your hands, ye shall give the Holy Ghost" (Moroni 2:2, emphasis added).

I can still remember Dave emphasizing the word "after"—it was after prayer that the ordinance was administered. He then read from the next chapter: "*After* they had prayed unto the Father in the name of Christ, they laid their hands upon them" (Moroni 3:2, emphasis added).

I have never forgotten the lesson taught to me that night, and I have tried in every situation since to pray with the person before laying hands on their head. I must have help to know what the Lord would have me say. I also believe a simple prayer before the blessing calms their heart. I know it certainly calms mine.

Two examples follow.

40 *The Doctor Says You're Dead*

Elder Matthew Cowley went to a hospital in New Zealand one day to bless a woman who was dying. She was having her farewell party. The Maori people have a wonderful view of death; they see death as the passing from one world to the next. They have the tradition of gathering around the person dying to celebrate their passing. They send messages to the other side: "When you get over there tell my mother I'm trying to do my best; I'm not so good, but I'm trying." "Tell her to have a good room fixed for me when I get over there and plenty of fish, good meals."

Elder Cowley's companion was the woman's uncle—nearly ninety years old. He stood at the head of the bed, and he said to his niece, "Vera, you're dead. You're dead because the doctor says you're dead. You're on your way out. . . . You're dead now, but you're going to live."

He turned to Elder Cowley and said, "Is it all right if we kneel down and pray?" Everybody in the room knelt, and after the prayer they blessed her.

The woman recovered completely—physically well from head to foot—and later had more children.[11]

11. Matthew Cowley, "Miracles," Brigham Young University devotional, Feb. 18, 1953, speeches.byu.edu.

41 *It Is Too Late*

Elder Lorenzo Snow sat at the bedside of an unconscious sailor—supposedly breathing his last breath. The dying man was a well-liked member of the crew and still very young. During the latter part of the voyage, he became sick and worsened day by day until death seemed inevitable. Members of the ship's crew came to take a farewell look at their lifeless companion and pay their final respects.

The ship was sailing from England to the United States and carried several Latter-day Saints immigrating to Zion. Elder Snow was returning from a mission to Europe. One of the Latter-day Saint women heard about the illness and told the ship's captain that Elder Snow could bless him to get better. The captain shook his head and said the man was breathing his last.

Elder Snow approached the captain anyway. Tearfully, the captain said, "Mr. Snow, it is too late; he is expiring." Elder Snow made no reply but sat by the dying man. He bowed his head in silent prayer and then laid his hands on the young man's head. In the name of Jesus Christ, he rebuked the disease and commanded him to be made whole.

To the astonishment of everyone on board, the young sailor soon walked the deck, praising and glorifying God. When the ship landed in New Orleans, several of the crew were baptized as members of The Church of Jesus Christ of Latter-day Saints.[12]

THE WILL OF GOD

I had an elder's quorum president some time ago whose faith was shaken to his very core. Mark had administered to an extremely ill fellow quorum member. In the blessing, he promised him that he would get better. He died that night.

12. Eliza R. Snow, *Biography and Family Record of Lorenzo Snow* (Salt Lake City: Deseret News Company, 1884), 65–66.

The next day was Sunday, and I remember him standing before our elder's quorum in tears, struggling to understand what had gone wrong. Why hadn't he been healed? "Why didn't the Lord honor my promises?"

> And whosoever among you are sick . . . the elders of the church, two or more, shall be called, and shall pray for and lay their hands upon them in my name; *and if they die* they shall die unto me, and if they live they shall live unto me.
>
> And it shall come to pass that those that die in me shall not taste of death, for it shall be sweet unto them;
>
> And again, it shall come to pass that he that hath faith in me to be healed, *and is not appointed unto death*, shall be healed. (Doctrine and Covenants 42:43–44, 46, 48)

This is why I always try to remember to pray before laying my hands on another person. I must know what God's will is for them. "All things are present with me, for I know them all," said the Lord to Moses (Moses 1:6). The Lord knows His children. He loves them, and He knows what is best for them. I must pray and listen to His promptings to know what His will is for them.

President Dallin H. Oaks taught, "We must always remember that faith and the healing power of the priesthood cannot produce a result contrary to the will of Him whose priesthood it is."[13]

42 *Let's See What the Lord Has in Mind*

Ted E. Brewerton was called as the mission president to the Costa Rica, San Jose Mission. While there, Sister Brewerton was diagnosed with a rare blood disorder. The disease had previously caused her to suffer two miscarriages, and she was threatening to miscarry again.

Marion G. Romney, then a member of the Quorum of the Twelve Apostles, toured their mission. When he learned of her problem, he said, "Let's see what the Lord has in mind." He laid his hands on her head.

13. Dallin H. Oaks, "Healing the Sick," *Ensign,* May 2010, 50.

President Brewerton remembered, "For a short time, he spoke to the Lord as one would to a close friend. Then he literally purged her system of the blood disease." The doctors could find no trace of the disease thereafter.

Sister Brewerton gave birth to a healthy baby girl, and three years later, she had a strong baby boy. The doctors continued to be clueless as to what happened; they had never heard of anyone being completely cured of this disease.[14]

WHY DO I NEED DOCTORS AND MEDICINES IF I CAN HAVE PRIESTHOOD BLESSINGS?

When someone requested a priesthood blessing from Brigham Young, he would often ask, "Have you used any remedies?"

If they said, "No, we wish the Elders to lay hands upon us, and we have faith that we shall be healed," President Young replied, "That is very inconsistent according to my faith. If we are sick, and ask the Lord to heal us, and to do all for us that is necessary to be done, according to my understanding of the Gospel of salvation, I might as well ask the Lord to cause my wheat and corn to grow without plowing the ground and casting in the seed. It appears consistent to me to apply every remedy that comes within the range of my knowledge, and [then] to ask my Father in Heaven . . . to sanctify that application healing to my body."[15]

President Thomas S. Monson called Jesus "The Great Physician."[16] The advancement of medical science in the past century has been nothing short of miraculous. Could not the Lord, "The Great Physician," have inspired many of these medical miracles to bless and help us?

Medical science is not at odds with the priesthood of God. The two may work in harmony in blessing the lives of countless people, but we must also do all that we can do and continue to call upon Heavenly Father for help and inspiration.

14. Derin Head Rodriguez, *From Every Nation* (Salt Lake City: Deseret Book, 1990), 92–93.
15. Young, Brigham, *Discourses of Brigham Young*, Compiled by John A. Widtsoe (Salt Lake City: Deseret Book, 1954), 163.
16. Thomas S. Monson, "Your Personal Influence," *Ensign,* May 2004, 23.

The following story illustrates how a woman was healed because of the inspiration her husband received while giving her a blessing. She was not healed directly because of the blessing, but the Lord told him what to do in order for her to be healed.

43 *I Know Now What You Are to Do*

When Joan Coombs's husband had been set apart as the mission president to Tonga, she too had been blessed with the gift of language, and within a year she was speaking fluent Tongan. She had immersed her home in the native culture, decorating it with beautiful artifacts, tapa cloths, wall hangings, and instruments.

Joan was eight months pregnant and deathly ill. Her lungs were filling with fluid and the doctors had no idea what was wrong. As her sickness increased, she found it increasingly difficult to breathe. She often had to sleep in a chair, as she couldn't breathe lying down.

Finally, her husband said, "The thing for us to do is to give you a blessing."

When he finished the blessing, she lay on her bed and got four hours of uninterrupted sleep. When she awoke, her husband said, "I know now what you are to do. The cause of your trouble is an allergy to the dyes that are in this house. We must take the tapas off the bed. We must take all these things out and put them in the back room. . . . We will keep them for gifts. Otherwise, you won't be able to get over this sickness."

They went to work. They took everything that might have been produced with Tongan dyes and placed them in a locked room.

Then he said, "The next thing you must do is to go to the doctor and ask him for an expectorant medicine that will force you to cough." She did, and for the next four days, she coughed up the phlegm in her lungs.[17]

17. Eric B. Shumway, *Tongan Saints: Legacy of Faith* (Institute for Polynesian Studies, 1991), 145–46.

All this inspiration came to President Coombs because of a priesthood blessing to his wife. The doctors didn't receive the inspiration, but they were able to help relieve the problem once the inspiration was received.

THE ROLE OF FAITH IN PRIESTHOOD ADMINISTRATIONS

Faith is essential before, during, and after the giving of priesthood blessings. Usually, we think of the faith of the priesthood holder giving the blessing combined with the faith of the person receiving the blessing. Occasionally, it is because of the faith of a third party.

Read these examples and look for whose faith was exhibited.

44 *How About Another Blessing?*

A desperate mother called Elder Matthew Cowley to the Salt Lake County hospital. Her boy was unconscious and dying from polio. She asked Elder Cowley to give him a blessing.

She said to him, "This is an unusual boy, not because he's my child, but he is an unusual boy."

As Elder Cowley laid his hands on the comatose boy, he could sense what his mother was saying. "I knew as I laid my hands upon that lad that he was an unusual boy, and that he had faith. Having faith in his faith, I blessed him to get well and promised him he would recover."

Elder Cowley dropped by the hospital a week later and asked if he could see the boy. The nurse said, "Certainly. Walk right down the hall."

A boy came running out to meet him and asked, "Are you Brother Cowley?"

"Yes."

"I want to thank you for that prayer. I was unconscious then, wasn't I?"

"You certainly were."

"That's the reason I don't recognize you. Come on in my room; I want to talk to you." He was an unusual boy.

They walked into his room. The boy still had a tube in his throat, so Elder Cowley said, "How long are you going to have that tube there?"

He said, "Oh, two weeks. Two more weeks and then I'm all well. How about another blessing?"

"Certainly." Elder Cowley laid his hands on the boy's head and blessed him again.

Elder Cowley started to leave, but the boy stopped him and asked, "Hey, how about my partner in the next bed?" There was a young man about sixteen or seventeen in the adjoining bed.

Elder Cowley said, "What do you mean?"

"Don't go out without blessing him. He's my partner."

"Sure."

Elder Cowley asked the young man, "Would you like a blessing?"

"Yes, sir. I'm a teacher in the Aaronic Priesthood in my ward."

Elder Cowley blessed him, and then he blessed another boy—another partner.[18]

45 *His Life Was Ebbing before Our Eyes*

Dr. Russell M. Nelson attended medical meetings at a resort hotel in a remote part of Mexico many years ago. Several of his colleagues in attendance were also members of The Church of Jesus Christ of Latter-day Saints. Suddenly, one of the physicians became seriously ill from massive bleeding in his stomach.

Under normal circumstances, any of the doctors present could have operated on the man and helped him but, as they watched their friend suffer, they realized they were helpless to save him. There was no hospital nearby and they did not have the necessary equipment to stop the bleeding or give transfusions. Because it was night, no planes could fly in or out of the resort.

"All the combined knowledge and concern there could not be converted to action to help our friend as we saw his life

18. Matthew Cowley, "Miracles," Brigham Young University devotional, Feb. 18, 1953, speeches.byu.edu.

ebbing before our eyes," said Dr. Nelson. "We were powerless to stop his bleeding."

The suffering doctor asked for a priesthood blessing. Several of the men holding the Melchizedek Priesthood immediately responded, and Dr. Nelson acted as the voice. "The Spirit dictated that the bleeding would stop and that the man would continue to live and return to his home and profession."

The man recovered and returned home.

When Dr. Nelson was called as an apostle of the Lord Jesus Christ, he said, "Men can do very little of themselves to heal sick or broken bodies. With an education, they can do a little more; with advanced medical degrees and training, a little more yet can be done. The real power to heal, however, is a gift from God. He has deigned that some of that power may be harnessed via the authority of his priesthood to benefit and bless mankind when all man can do for himself may not be sufficient."[19]

46 *Bless the Pain Away*

The Provo Missionary Training Center (MTC) is usually a beehive of activity 365 days a year. For each missionary, no time can be wasted if they are to take advantage of the few weeks they have for training, especially if that training involves learning a foreign language.

One evening, a young elder studying Japanese cried out in pain. He had a terrible toothache, and his jaw was so swollen he had been unable to eat anything all day. He couldn't see a dentist until the following day and cried out for someone to help him.

His MTC branch president happened to be in a meeting nearby and was called out to meet with the elder. The missionary asked him if he would "bless the pain away."

"Do you think it can be done?" the branch president asked. He was already thinking of how he could get the elder some pain pills until he could see the dentist the next day.

19. Marvin K. Gardner, "Elder Russell M. Nelson: Applying Divine Laws," *Ensign*, June 1984, 8–13.

With great faith, the elder said, "I know the Lord can do it, and I don't see any useful lesson to be gained by this pain when I can't concentrate on Japanese or anything but this pain; and I see a whole lot to be gained if the Lord will simply stop the pain."

The Spirit whispered to the branch president what he should say in the blessing. He promised the elder that he would be healed at once. That was Thursday evening.

He didn't see the elder again until Sunday morning when the elder came to his office door "bright-eyed and radiant" to tell his branch president of the miracle that had happened. Within minutes of the blessing Thursday night, the pain had stopped. Within the next hour, the throbbing ceased. By the time he got back to his room, the swelling had left, and he was able to eat. He did not keep his appointment with the dentist the next afternoon; he said he couldn't afford the time away from Japanese. "He bore testimony to me that his joy in the reality of the Holy Spirit in his life exceeded the relief he experienced with the cessation of pain."[20]

THEY ARE A REALITY

Before Jesus left His apostles for the last time after His resurrection and ascended into heaven, He told them, "Go ye into all the world, and preach the gospel to every creature. . . . And these signs shall follow them that believe; . . . they shall lay hands on the sick, and they shall recover" (Mark 16:15–18). The last verse of the chapter then says, "And they went forth . . . the Lord working *with* them" (Mark 16:20, emphasis added).

I testify that the Lord still works with us today. He continues to inspire righteous priesthood holders as they administer to the sick and the afflicted, and He continues to honor the promises they make when under His inspiration.

President Spencer W. Kimball wrote to the youth of the Church in 1983 about administering to the sick. He bore this testimony: "Let

20. Richard H. Cracroft, "'We'll Sing and We'll Shout:' A Mantic Celebration of the Holy Spirit," Brigham Young University devotional, June 29, 1993, 131.

not the skeptic disturb your faith in these miraculous healings. They are numerous. They are sacred. Many volumes would not hold them. They are simple and complex. They are gradual, and they are instantaneous. They are a reality."[21]

I conclude this chapter with two more stories that testify of this reality.

47 *There Are No Scars*

David O. McKay was a very young man when he was called to be an apostle in 1906. Forty-five years later he became the ninth president of The Church of Jesus Christ of Latter-day Saints, but he almost didn't live that long.

In 1916, David was in a horrible car accident that nearly took his life, or, at the very least, nearly disfigured him for life.

The Ogden River overflowed in March 1916, causing widespread flooding and destruction. The bridge at the mouth of the canyon became unstable and was closed for safety reasons. The watchman guarding the bridge left at seven o'clock and stretched a large rope across the entrance to warn cars not to pass.

Coming down the canyon, David McKay and his brother, Thomas, did not see the rope until it was too late. Thomas yelled, "Oh, look out! There's a rope!"

David reached for the emergency brake, but it was too late. The rope smashed the window and drew back the top of the car. Thomas was able to duck and escaped without injury, but the rope caught David in the chin, severing his lip, knocking out his lower teeth, and breaking his jaw. He was knocked unconscious.

Within two hours, David was on the operating table, the doctors trying their best to repair his face. One of the attendants remarked, "Too bad. He will be disfigured for life."

When he was wheeled to his hospital room, one of the nurses consolingly remarked, "Well, Brother McKay, you can wear a beard," meaning that it might hide his scars.

---

21. Spencer W. Kimball, "President Kimball Speaks Out on Administration to the Sick," *New Era,* Oct. 1981, 50.

He received a priesthood blessing. In sealing the anointing, he was told, "We bless you that you shall not be disfigured and that you shall not have pain."

On Sunday morning, his quorum president, Heber J. Grant, drove from Salt Lake City to see Elder McKay. When he entered the hospital room, he said, "David, don't talk. I'm just going to give you a blessing."

Seven months later, Elder David O. McKay was seated across a table from President Grant, who looked at him intently and then said, "David, from where I am sitting, I cannot see a scar on your face!"

"No, President Grant, there are no scars."[22]

48 Do You Remember the Promises You Made?

"Do you remember me?" she asked.

"You are Sister Frenzel." Frederick Babbel remembered her from his mission to Germany six years previously.

"Do you remember the promises you made to me when you blessed me just before you left Nuremburg in 1939 to return home?"

He could never forget those promises. Sister Frenzel had been expecting her first child although she was then in her forties. Her health was tenuous, and the doctor had expressed concern that she might lose her own life, as well as the child. She and her crippled husband had converted a little garden shed into a one-room home. It would be difficult to bring a child home under such circumstances.

Elder Babbel and his companion laid their hands on Sister Frenzel's head and began pronouncing the words of the blessing. Partway through, he stopped, unable to believe the promises he was making to her. He blessed her that she would have a son (there were no sonograms to detect the sex of the baby in

22. David O. McKay, *Cherished Experiences, from the Writings of President David O. McKay,* compiled by Clare Middlemiss (Salt Lake City: Deseret Book, 1955), 148.

those days). "I was concerned that I had committed a serious mistake," said Elder Babbel.

The promises kept coming. The boy "would grow up to receive the priesthood and become a leader in the Church." It was as if he couldn't stop his mouth from making incredible promises to her. "I promised her that she should have no serious pain in childbirth and that because of her faith she should yet rear a large family." Elder Babbel was incredulous. How could this possibly come true; she was already in her forties and the doctors feared for her life with this child?

Oh yes, he remembered the promises. It was now nearly seven years later. She stood before him and said, "I would like to have you meet my family." Four children stood before him. The oldest, a boy, she had named Frederick William after Elder Babbel.[23]

23. Frederick William Babbel, *On Wings of Faith* (Salt Lake City: Bookcraft, 1972), 63–64.

Chapter 6

Divine Protection

"But thou, O Lord, art a shield for me."
Psalms 3:3

---

49 *The Empty Choir Loft*

Choir practice began at 7:20 sharp every Wednesday evening at the West Side Baptist church in Beatrice, Nebraska. "I can't remember a time when anybody came late," said Marilyn, the choir pianist. However, on March 1, 1950, *everyone* was late.

Pastor Walter Kempel had gone to the church earlier in the day to get things ready for rehearsal. It was a cold day, so he lit the furnace and went home for dinner.

The choir director, Mrs. Paul, was always at least fifteen minutes early. She demanded that her choir members be punctual as well, but on March 1st when it was time to leave, she discovered that her daughter had lain down for a nap. By the time she was ready to go, they were late—their first time.

Including Mrs. Paul, there were fifteen members of the West Side Baptist Church choir. Never before, or since, has every member of the choir been late for rehearsal.

They all had valid excuses. The pastor, his wife, and daughter Marilyn were late because Marilyn had stained her dress, and Mrs. Kempel had to iron a new one for her to wear.

Two high school students who usually rode together were late because one just had to listen to the exciting end of a half-hour radio program that had begun at 7:00 p.m.

Two other women were late when their car wouldn't start; they had to call for a ride from another member who was also running late.

Ordinarily, Mrs. Schuster was ten minutes early for choir practice. The night of March 1st she was detained at her mother's house; the two were preparing for a later missionary meeting.

Herb had an important letter he had to write. He had been putting it off for too long and the time just got away from him.

Harvey would have been on time, but his wife was out of town, and she had left him in charge of their two young sons.

Joyce Black would probably not have been early though she would have been on time. It was just so cold out that night that she wanted to wait until the last possible minute. Besides, she just lived across the street from the church. It would only take a minute to walk over.

All fifteen members had valid reasons for being late. Not one person was at the church for the 7:30 rehearsal.

March 1, 1950, at exactly 7:25 p.m., a natural gas leak surfaced in the basement of the church and was ignited by the old furnace. The West Side Baptist Church was demolished. The old furnace was located directly below the choir loft—the empty choir loft.[1]

1. It was *Paul Harvey's The Rest of the Story* (Bantam Books, 1978) that first drew my attention to this story. I found a 60th anniversary new article remembering the story in 2010 (Luke Nichols, "Remember the miracle," *Beatrice Daily Sun,* Mar. 1, 2010). *Snopes.com* has also proven the story true ("Church Explosion Spares Choir," *Snopes.com*, Dec. 31, 1998, https://www.snopes.com/fact-check/choir-non-quorum/).

THE GOSPEL AS A BULWARK

Christians all over the world sing the majestic hymn, "A mighty fortress is our God, a tower of strength ne'er failing." When Martin Luther originally wrote that hymn, he used the word "bulwark" instead of tower. A bulwark is a defensive wall used by ancient peoples to protect themselves from their enemies. I think Martin Luther was trying to convey the message that our God, omniscient and omnipotent as He is, has the power and ability to protect us from our enemies both seen and unseen.

"There are physical and spiritual dangers for Latter-day Saints and their loved ones," President Henry B. Eyring told a Women's Conference in 2013. "We will need divine protection in our journey through this last dispensation as it moves toward its climactic end."[2]

The scriptures are full of metaphors for God as our protector. "The Lord is my rock, and my fortress and my deliverer; my God, my strength . . . my buckler" (Psalms 18:2). A buckler is a type of shield. "I will be their shield and their buckler; and I will gird up their loins . . . and their enemies shall be under their feet; and I will let fall the sword in their behalf, and by the fire of mine indignation will I preserve them" (Doctrine and Covenants 35:14). "Fear not, Abram: I am thy shield" (Genesis 15:1).

50 *Give Up Mormonism or I'll Shoot You*

My children's third-great grandfather, Benjamin F. Johnson, was a friend and bodyguard to the prophet Joseph Smith. Benjamin's loyalty to Joseph was tested in Missouri when the Latter-day Saints were driven from the state.

Benjamin was taken prisoner by the mob. One of the guards walked up to him and said, "Give up Mormonism right now, or I'll shoot you."

Benjamin, faithful since his baptism, refused. The guard stood ten feet away, took direct aim with his rifle and pulled the trigger. Nothing happened.

2. Sarah Jane Weaver, "President Eyring Speaks of Divine Protection at Conference," *Church News,* May 8, 2013.

He swore and said, "I have used this gun for twenty years and it has never misfired before." He examined the lock, reloaded the rifle, aimed again, and pulled the trigger. Still nothing; a third time produced the same result.

One last time he loaded the gun, took direct aim at Benjamin and fired. This time there was an explosion, but the gun burst and killed the mobster.[3]

WE CAN ASK FOR DIVINE PROTECTION

Heavenly Father wants so much to bless us, but sometimes waits for us to seek His help. "Whosoever shall call on the name of the Lord shall be delivered" (Joel 2:32).

The word "supplicate" or "supplication" is found in scripture fifty-two times. The definition comes from the Latin prefix "*sub*" meaning from below and "*placer*" meaning propitiate or to implore. To supplicate then is to humbly implore. "For the Nephites did not fear them; but they did fear their God and did supplicate him for protection" (3 Nephi 4:10). The rest of this chapter from the Book of Mormon tells how the Nephites were able to defeat the Gadianton Robbers. When the evil leader Zemnarihah was hanged, the people cried out to God in gratitude, "May the God of Abraham, and the God of Isaac, and the God of Jacob, protect this people in righteousness, so long as they shall call on the name of their God for protection" (3 Nephi 4:30).

There is the key: they had to ask. Here are three stories of those who supplicated the Lord for divine protection.

51 *Bringing Them All Home Alive*

An estimated 100,000 members of The Church of Jesus Christ of Latter-day Saints served in the military during World War II. Sadly, 5,000 did not come home alive. Many who survived humbly testified of divine intervention. Charles Henry was one.

Charles fasted and prayed that he "might have the guidance and help necessary" to keep the men under his command

3. "Chapter Four: Establishing Zion in Missouri," *Our Heritage: A Brief History of The Church of Jesus Christ of Latter-day Saints* (Salt Lake City: The Church of Jesus Christ of Latter-day Saints, 1996).

safe and able to accomplish their mission. "I even asked Him if I might be granted the blessing of bringing them all home alive." He wept as he prayed, feeling peace and comfort.

The American and British military had pushed the German army out of France since June 6, 1944—D-Day. On October 2nd, the infantry was ordered to cross the Wurm River in Germany.

Charles briefed his men at 9:00 p.m. the night before and suggested they relax and get some sleep. He would waken them at 6:00 a.m. the next morning. He sincerely prayed before falling asleep.

About 1:00 in the morning, he was awakened by a voice: "Arouse the men and move them into the school basement." Thinking he had been dreaming, he ignored the voice and went back to sleep, but the warning came a second time: "Arouse the men and move them into the school basement."

He again ignored the voice and went back to sleep. About 1:30 a.m., "it seemed that someone grasped my shoulders, shook me awake, and demanded that I get those men up." This time he acted immediately.

As the last man entered the schoolhouse, German artillery blanketed the area. The place where his men had been sleeping was destroyed.

Commander Henry gathered his men in the school basement and told them of his prayers and warnings. "The men were very touched and promised that if I would always follow those promptings they would never complain, nor question any order given them." Before dismissing the men, Charles offered a prayer of gratitude, and many tears were shed.[4]

52 *Why Can't I Bless This House?*

The country of Tonga was slammed by a major cyclone in 1961 with winds up to 150 miles per hour. Fifty percent of the homes were demolished or badly damaged—8,000 people

4. Robert C. Freeman and Dennis A. Wright, *Saints at War: Experiences of Latter-day Saints in World War II* (Salt Lake City: Covenant Communications, 2001), 134–35.

left homeless. The banana crop was completely wiped out and 10,000 coconut trees were destroyed.

Tonga Pōteki Mālohifo'ou, and his wife, Ana, were faithful Latter-day Saints who survived the cyclone through a modern-day miracle.

The ferocious tropical cyclone hit on March 16,1961. Tonga, Ana, and their family watched in horror through their living room window at the destruction happening all around them. Homes and trees were being torn apart and flung through the air. One home was lifted off its foundation. A Protestant church across the road crumbled into a heap.

Their own home was shaking violently, the tin roof "groaning" as if ready to tear asunder. The family was terrified. Tonga reminded them that they had already had their evening prayers and tried to comfort them by saying that the Lord would not forsake them.

"A strange idea came into my mind," Tonga recalled. "If I can heal the sick with a priesthood blessing, why can't I bless this house and stop the wind from destroying it?"

He stood on his bed, reached up toward the rafters, and gave their house a blessing: "By virtue of the holy Melchizedek Priesthood vested in me and in the name of Jesus Christ, I command this roof to stay exactly where you are! Do not move even one degree. Also, to the roof over the kitchen, to every piece of lumber and sheet of tin in this house, and to the unfallen trees outside in the yard, I command you to stand solidly where you are!"

From that very moment the house quit shaking, and the roof stopped trembling. They felt peace throughout the night. In the morning the storm had subsided, and they ventured outside to see the incredible damage around them. Their neighbors looked at Tonga's and Ana's house in amazement—it was still intact.[5]

5. Eric B. Shumway, *Tongan Saints: Legacy of Faith* (Institute for Polynesian Studies, 1991), 226–28.

53 *A Stop Sign Right in Front of My Eyes*

The state of Oklahoma has an average of fifty-two tornadoes every year. The tornado that struck the Oklahoma City area on May 20, 2013 was particularly devastating. Twenty-four people were killed and thousands of structures were leveled.

Tori Sorrels, a fifth grader at Plaza Towers Elementary School, recounts how she was miraculously protected.

Tori and several of her friends huddled in a school bathroom when the category E5 tornado descended upon their school. "I heard something hit the roof. I thought it was just hailing. The sound got louder and louder. I said a prayer that Heavenly Father would protect us all and keep us safe. All of a sudden we heard a loud vacuum sound, and the roof disappeared right above our heads. There was lots of wind and debris flying around and hitting every part of my body. It was darker outside and it looked like the sky was black, but it wasn't—it was the inside of the tornado."

Tori closed her eyes and continued praying. Suddenly it was quiet. "When I opened my eyes, I saw a stop sign right in front of my eyes. It was almost touching my nose."

Elder Ronald A. Rasband, then of the Presidency of the Seventy, visited with Tori and her family a week after the disaster. He asked if he could give her a blessing before he left. As he laid his hands on her head, a scripture came to his mind: "I will go before your face. I will be on your right hand and on your left, and my Spirit shall be in your hearts, and mine angels round about you, to bear you up" (Doctrine and Covenants 84:88).

Elder Rasband counseled Tori "to remember the day when a servant of the Lord laid his hands on her head and pronounced that she had been protected by angels in the storm."[6]

6. Ronald A. Rasband, "The Joyful Burden of Discipleship," *Ensign*, May 2014, 11.

SPECIAL PROTECTION FOR THE LORD'S SERVANTS

"No weapon that is formed against thee shall prosper; . . . This is the heritage of the servants of the Lord" (Isaiah 54:17). Divine protections are given to those whom God has given special assignments until their mission is complete. Thus, Abinadi was protected from the wicked King Noah until he had delivered the message God told him to deliver (Mosiah 13–17).

Lorenzo Snow was divinely protected many times during his 52-year apostolic ministry. His patriarchal blessing promised him, "Thou hast a great work to perform in thy day and generation. . . . There shall not be a mightier man on earth than thou. Thou shalt have long life. The vigor of thy mind shall not be abated and the vigor of thy body shall be preserved." His life was preserved on more than one occasion.[7]

Here is an example from the life of Lorenzo Snow that shows that divine protection, followed by another story about a modern-day prophet, President Russell M. Nelson.

54 *Arrangements to Mob Me*

Lorenzo Snow was 22 years old when he joined The Church of Jesus Christ of Latter-day Saints in Kirtland, Ohio. Less than one year later, he served his first mission in and around Mantua, Ohio—his birthplace.

"I dreamed one night that arrangements were in progress to mob me," Lorenzo later told his sister, Eliza.

The next day, a loud knock was heard at his door. Two well-dressed strangers entered and invited Elder Snow to preach to a congregation that had assembled at the local schoolhouse, only about a mile distant.

Lorenzo hesitated and the strangers became rather insistent that he come. Suddenly, the dream he had the night before flashed before his mind. Lorenzo told them he could not go with them.

7. Arthur R. Bassett, "The Prophet of the Lord," *New Era*, Jan. 1972.

The strangers now became angry, but Lorenzo continued to hold fast that he would not go. The next day he learned that those gathered at the schoolhouse had no intention of listening to Elder Snow preach but to do him harm. Lorenzo had been divinely protected.[8]

55 *The Armed Robbers Had One Intention*

Members of the Quorum of the Twelve have an apostolic duty to take the gospel to the ends of the earth. I doubt there is a country on this earth where an apostle of the Lord has not set his feet at one time or another.

President Russell M. Nelson and his wife Wendy had gone to Mozambique, Africa in 2009 to visit with the Saints and conduct Church business.

While having dinner with the mission president and his wife, armed thugs stormed into the home and attacked them. "The four armed robbers had one intention," Sister Nelson said, "to kill my husband, and to take me hostage." She felt a comforting peace that helped her remain calm during the attack.

One of the men pointed his gun at Elder Nelson's head and pulled the trigger. The gun failed to fire. Sister Nelson was suddenly released from their grasp, and the men scattered.

President Nelson said, "We were mercifully rescued from potential disaster. We know we were protected by angels round about us."[9]

---

8. Eliza Roxey Snow Smith, *Biography and Family Record of Lorenzo Snow* (Salt Lake City: Deseret News Company, 1884), 17. See also, Francis M. Gibbons, *Lorenzo Snow: Spiritual Giant, Prophet of God* (Salt Lake City: Deseret Book, 1982), 14–15.
9. Russell M. Nelson, *Accomplishing the Impossible* (Salt Lake City: Deseret Book, 2015), 25; see also Sharon Haddock, "Apostle's wife felt comfort despite attack," *Deseret News*, Nov. 15, 2009.

THE MIRACULOUS POWER OF GOD

I love the Book of Mormon story of the stripling warriors. It was an absolute miracle that all 2,060 survived every battle they fought. Their leader, Helaman, described "their preservation" as "astonishing to our whole army," but took no credit for himself. "And we do justly ascribe it to the miraculous power of God, because of their exceeding faith in that which they had been taught to believe—that there was a just God, and whosoever did not doubt, that they should be preserved by his marvelous power" (Alma 57:26).

The modern-day army of young men and women and senior couples who serve full-time missions for the Lord's church are also miraculously preserved. President Dallin Oaks, spoke to a group of young adults and said, "Still another miracle is the way missionaries are protected during their labors. Of course, we have fatalities among our young missionaries—about three to six per year over the last decade—all of them tragic. But the official death rates for comparable-age young men and women in the United States are eight times higher than the death rates of our missionaries. In other words, our young men and women are eight times safer in the mission field than the general population of their peers at home. In view of the hazards of missionary labor, this mortality record is nothing less than a miracle."[10]

We will conclude this chapter with a modern-day miracle about the preservation of an entire mission in Japan.

56 *The Lord Had Moved Them to Safe Ground*

Disaster struck Japan on March 11, 2011. The largest earthquake in Japan's history hit without warning at 2:46 p.m. The epicenter of the 9.1 magnitude earthquake was 231 miles northeast of Tokyo near Sendai. The resulting tsunami caused 30-foot waves that wiped out entire communities and damaged several nuclear reactors. More than 16,000 people were killed with thousands more still missing.

---

10. Dallin H. Oaks, "Miracles," *Ensign*, June 2001.

Not one missionary in the Japan Sendai Mission was killed or hurt.

The mission president, Reid Tateoka, had planned a leadership meeting on March 11, 2011 in Koriyama, an inland city 79 miles south of Sendai.

"A few days prior to the meeting, President Tateoka had an impression, a feeling in his heart, to invite *all* missionaries of that zone to the leadership meeting instead of the prescribed small number of elder and sister leaders."[11]

The massive earthquake struck Japan during the meeting, but all the missionaries were far away from the epicenter. "The Lord had moved them to safe ground."[12]

11. Gary E. Stevenson, "How Does the Holy Ghost Help You?" *Ensign*, May 2017, 119.
12. Reid Tateoka, "He Would Deliver Us," *Ensign*, February 2018.

Chapter 7

Sacred Dreams

"God came to Abimelech in a dream by night."
Genesis 20:3

---

57 What Happened to That Dishrag?

Vickie and I had only been married a few months when we experienced an answer to our prayers given through a simple dream.

We lived in an apartment, part of an old house owned by an elderly woman. She was very frugal; that explains why she controlled the thermostat to the heater, and also explains why it was always so cold in our apartment.

We were students at Brigham Young University in our last year and were dirt poor. We were both working part-time while attending school full-time. I remember Elder M. Russell Ballard once saying to a group of young adults that they should "not miss living through difficult times with [their] companion."[1] Vickie and I didn't miss a thing.

I came home from work earlier than normal one late autumn evening; Vickie wouldn't be home for a couple hours.

1. M. Russell Ballard, "Keep the Commandments—Beginning Right Now!" Brigham Young University fireside, Sept. 6, 1987, speeches.byu.edu.

When I walked into the kitchen and saw that the dishes needed to be done, I thought I would be a wonderful, thoughtful, and considerate husband and clean the kitchen before she arrived home. Wouldn't she be surprised?

Of course, there was no automatic dishwasher. I wasn't even sure electricity had been invented when this old house was built. The sink was wide and deep and required a plug that had to be inserted by hand. After placing the plug, I filled the sink with hot, soapy water and commenced to place all the dirty dishes inside. Located next to the old sink was a drawer where we kept dishrags and towels. One dishrag should do the trick. I then went to work.

Just as I finished cleaning the last dish, the doorbell rang. "I wonder who that could be this late," I thought to myself. I took my hands out of the dish water with the intent of drying them before answering the door when I thought, "You might as well pull the plug to the sink while your hands are still wet." I did and ran into the living room.

I can't even remember who was at the door that night, but I remember conversing with him for several minutes before returning to the kitchen and seeing that the kitchen table needed to be wiped off. "No problem," I thought to myself while walking to the kitchen sink, "I'll just grab the dishrag I just used to clean the dishes and . . ."

The dishrag was not in the sink.

"Hmmm. I wonder what I did with that dish rag." I looked all around the kitchen; it was nowhere to be found. I walked back to the living room thinking I may have taken it with me when I answered the door—not there either.

"What happened to that dish rag?" I said out loud.

After scratching my head for another minute, I got another dishrag out of the drawer and wiped off the kitchen table. I was looking over my handiwork with pride when I heard the front door open and Vickie walked in. She took one look at the kitchen and gave me a big hug. It was all worth it.

The next morning, Saturday, Vickie fixed a wonderful breakfast and then proceeded to do the dishes. She went through the entire process I had the prior evening, but this time when she pulled the plug to the sink, nothing happened; it wouldn't drain.

"Jon," she called to me, "Something's wrong with the sink. Can you come and see if you can fix it?"

Now, I am no handy man, but I had watched enough television to know that, when your sink is plugged, you need what we used to call a "plumber's helper." We happened to have a plunger in the bathroom, so I grabbed it and went to work on the clogged sink.

Nothing. It wouldn't drain.

What next? According to all the television commercials I watched growing up, I should get Drano. So, I hopped in the car and bought a large bottle at a local grocery store.

Upon returning to the scene of the crime, I took a few minutes to carefully read the instructions: "pour one cup down the clogged drain, wait for 30 minutes, flush." Sounds easy enough.

I poured. I waited. I flushed. Nothing!

"Maybe now the plunger will work," I thought to myself as I went back to my original plan. Nope.

So, I poured another cup of Drano down the sink. Again I waited, flushed, and got the same result. Again, I plunged—still nothing.

I became increasingly frustrated. I knew we didn't have enough money for a plumber, and I knew that our landlady would be of no help.

Out of pure exasperation, I poured the rest of the bottle of Drano down the sink. I waited. I flushed. I plunged. I fumed. The sink was still clogged. I had spent almost my entire Saturday on that stupid sink, and when it was time to go to bed, it was still clogged.

Fortunately, Vickie and I had established a habit of family prayer in our young marriage. We knelt by the side of our bed each evening and took turns expressing gratitude and imploring God for his blessings upon us.

I remember very well that it was my turn to say the prayer that Saturday evening, but I was in no mood to pray. I said, "Vickie, you pray."

She looked at me, and then she very humbly bowed her head and began a very simple, heartfelt petition. "Heavenly Father, our sink is broken. Please help us fix our sink, in the name of Jesus Christ. Amen."

The next morning, I was getting ready for Church and putting my tie on, when she rolled over in bed and said to me, "Jon, I just had the strangest dream. I dreamed there was a dishrag caught in our sink."

It was like a light bulb suddenly appeared over my head. "That's what happened to the dishrag!" I immediately knew she was right.

I went to the bedroom closet and found an old wire hanger. After twisting and straightening it, I pushed it down the clogged sink and pulled out the dishrag—half eaten by Drano.

I learned a valuable lesson that weekend: the power of prayer is real. I also learned that our prayers can be answered in unusual ways, such as sacred dreams.

THE FRUIT OF FAITH

"Inspired dreams are the fruit of faith," said Elder Bruce R. McConkie.[2] As was just evidenced, my wife had faith and had an inspired dream as a result.

The Bible dictionary teaches that dreams are "one of the means by which God communicates with men."[3] Not all dreams are revelations, but I believe they are one way that Heavenly Father can communicate with us. Elder James E. Talmage confirmed that revelations could come "through the dreams of sleep or in waking visions of the mind."[4] President Spencer W. Kimball taught, "Some revelations come by

2. Bruce R. McConkie, *Mormon Doctrine*, 2nd ed. (Salt Lake City: Bookcraft, 1966), 208.
3. Bible Dictionary, "Dreams," 659.
4. James E Talmage, *The Articles of Faith*, 12th ed. (Salt Lake City: The Church of Jesus Christ of Latter-day Saints, 1924), 229.

dreams. Most of our dreams are flighty and have no meaning, but the Lord does use dreams for enlightening his people."[5]

How do you know when you have an inspired dream? I can't speak for everyone, least of all prophets who have recorded some of their dreams in scripture, but for me, when I have an inspired dream, I wake up feeling the Spirit. I can usually remember the dream vividly, and I lay in bed pondering the significance of the message. It will usually be a message of something I need to change in my life, or something that I need to do. Many times, I feel the Spirit so strongly that I don't want to move for fear that the dream and the Spirit I feel will leave.

President Wilford Woodruff said, "There are a great many things taught us in dreams that are true, and if a man has the spirit of God, he can tell the difference between what is from the Lord and what is not."[6]

Here is an example from my personal life when I felt the Holy Spirit during a dream, and I knew I needed to act.

58 *My Three Grandfathers*

I grew up with three grandfathers. My father's parents were divorced and remarried ten years before I was born, so I grew up thinking everyone had three sets of grandparents. None of them were members of The Church of Jesus Christ of Latter-day Saints; my mother and I were the first to join the Church.

By 1994, all three of my grandfathers had died. All three of my grandmothers were still alive but would pass on a few years later.

One night in 1994, I dreamed that one of my grandfather's came to me. When I saw him, I started to run from him. I then thought to myself, "Why am I running from my grandfather? I love him," so I turned around. He came to me and hugged me; I could actually feel the warmth of his embrace

5. Spencer W. Kimball, *The Teachings of Spencer W. Kimball*, Edited by Edward L. Kimball (Salt Lake City: Bookcraft, 1982), 455.
6. Wilford Woodruff, *The Discourses of Wilford Woodruff*, sel. G. Homer Durham (Salt Lake City: Bookcraft, 1946), 285–86.

and see the smile on his face. I felt his unconditional love for me, and oh how I loved him. The dream ended.

I lay in bed pondering why I had that particular dream. I could strongly feel the Spirit's sweet presence.

A few nights later, I had the same dream except with a different grandfather. Again, when I saw him, I ran, then turned around and embraced him. Again, I felt his warm embrace and our complete love for each other. As I awoke, the Spirit warmed me, and I knew I'd had a sacred dream, but what did it mean?

A few nights later, came the last dream. This time my third grandfather came. It was the same dream and the same result as before, with one exception.

This time when I woke, I knew what the three dreams meant. As I lay pondering, the Spirit testified to me that I needed to do my grandfathers' temple work. None of them had been members of the Lord's Church although all three had been good men. I knew that they would accept the gospel in the spirit world, now it was up to me to have their vicarious work done for them.

I went to my local family history center and learned how easy it was to submit names for temple work. On October 29, 1994, I took my oldest son, Jamen, to the Denver Temple and baptized and confirmed him in behalf of my three grandfathers.

THE DREAM WAS DOUBLED

Joseph was brought before the pharaoh of Egypt to interpret the pharaoh's troubling dreams. Pharaoh had two similar dreams. Joseph explained, "And for that *the dream was doubled* unto Pharaoh twice; it is because the thing is established by God, and God will shortly bring it to pass" (Genesis 41:32, emphasis added).

This is another way one can know that their personal dreams might be inspired by God. As in the previous story, I not only felt the Spirit very strongly, but the dream was also repeated, in my case, three times before I finally got the message. Here are some other examples of dreams that were doubled.

59 *Their Mobile Home Was Engulfed in Flames*

Patricia and her husband had just moved to a small town in southern Georgia with their three small children. He had graduated from college and had obtained employment there. They felt lucky to have found a small two-bedroom mobile home to live in. The trailer had been vacant for some time.

One night, Patricia dreamed that their mobile home was engulfed in flames. When she had the same dream a second time, she woke frightened with a sense of foreboding. She recalled a phrase from her patriarchal blessing: "You will be warned of the approach of evil and be protected from harm and accident." She knew they had to move.

Supported by her husband, Patricia searched all over town and found a small three-bedroom house to move to.

One week later she received a phone call. "Have you heard? The trailer you lived in burned to the ground today."[7]

It wasn't until Patricia had her dream a second time that she felt compelled to act. Perhaps that is why the Lord repeats dreams—to get our attention. The following two stories are also dreams that have been doubled; however, the same dreams were given to different persons.

60 *Both Had the Same Dream*

Imagine the odds of two people having the exact same dream, at the exact same time. That is precisely what happened to Dennis and Geri Walton.

Early one morning, Dennis and Geri simultaneously awoke and were amazed to discover that they had both dreamed about being in a hospital delivery room in the late stages of labor. In the dream a tiny baby girl was born to them, smaller than the rest of their children; their previous four children had been delivered by cesarean section.

7. Patricia Tarrant, "Forewarned by a Dream," *Ensign*, March 1993, 64–65.

Dennis and Geri excitedly talked about their new baby girl as if Geri had truly just given birth to her. They were concerned about her small size, but impressed with what a beautiful baby girl she was.

Nine days later, the phone rang at their home. Geri answered it. The caller was from the Social Services Department. "I know that it's unusual to bother our foster families on a weekend, but we have an emergency situation and need some help. We have a baby that has to be moved from a hospital nursery this morning. She's rather ill, quite small, and . . . she's been under observation for the last week or so. However, she's no longer considered to be at intense risk. . . . Basically, we require a home that can observe her for a week or so before we place her for adoption."

"How old is this baby?" Geri asked.

"Let's see. . . . She's about nine days old."

Geri's heart leaped and tears came to her eyes as she told the social worker, "What time would you like to drop the baby off?"

She ran to Dennis, still crying, and told him about the baby.

When they met their new baby girl, Stacey, she looked exactly as they had seen in their dreams.

Stacey had many health problems to overcome and continued to stay with the Walton family until her final adoption papers were completed over two years later. Shortly thereafter, Stacey was sealed to Dennis and Geri Walton in the Alberta, Canada Temple.[8]

61 *A White Man to Come among Them*

Elder Melvin J. Ballard was serving as the mission president of the Northwestern States Mission in the early 1910s. One day while crossing Montana by train, the train approached a small town under development. Elder Ballard noticed an encampment nearby of several hundred Native Americans;

8. Geri Walton, "A Special Baby, a Dream Fulfilled," *Ensign*, September 1986.

their teepees were pitched in a large circle. Suddenly, Elder Ballard felt impressed to get off the train and visit them. He made arrangements to be picked up the next day.

As he walked among the Native American encampment, they became excited and emotional. They started talking to him in their language with great excitement and seemed to be asking him for something.

Elder Ballard's interpreter explained that many of the Native Americans had dreamed of a tall white man coming among them with books that would be of great value to their people. As soon as they saw Elder Ballard, they recognized him as the man in their dreams, and they wanted the books he was supposed to bring.

Elder Ballard taught them about the Book of Mormon and of its significance to them. He told them he must go away but that he would return with the books.

Many of these Native Americans joined the Church, and today many of their descendants are firm in the faith of the gospel.[9]

DREAMS MAY BE GIVEN TO PREPARE OR FOREWARN

Mary had delivered the promised Messiah in Bethlehem as was prophesied. Soon after the visit of the wise men, Joseph had a troubling dream that they must leave Bethlehem at once and flee to Egypt. He was obedient, and thus Jesus was saved from the evil edict of Herod (Matthew 2:13–14).

Lehi was warned in a dream from the Lord to flee from Jerusalem (1 Nephi 2:1–2). He was obedient, and thus his family was saved, and an entire civilization was begun. We reap the benefits today from their written records.

In the decade preceding the birth of the Prophet Joseph Smith, his father received seven sacred dreams preparing him for the great work his son would begin. No wonder when Joseph went to his father to tell

9. Melvin J. Ballard, *Melvin J. Ballard, Crusader for Righteousness* (Salt Lake City: Bookcraft, 1966), 55–57.

him of the angel's visitation, Joseph Smith Sr. replied, "It is of God" (Joseph Smith—History 1:49–50).

Sometimes the warnings may not be because of mortal danger but to prepare us for future events.

62 *I Will Drown in the River*

David was hired to rebuild a cabin in a mountain canyon not too far from his home. Located in a picturesque setting, the cabin stood along the banks of a beautiful stream. When the weather was warmer, David began taking his two-and-a-half-year-old son, Kenny, with him. The boy kept himself entertained for hours exploring the area, fascinated by the animals and throwing rocks and sticks into the fast-moving water. His father always kept a watchful eye on him, but little Kenny seemed to grow ever more confident in his beautiful surroundings.

After about a month, David had a terrible dream that made him wake up in a cold sweat. He dreamed that Kenny fell into the stream and drowned. The dream seemed so real that he was left shaken and knew that his dream was a warning. He wouldn't be able to take Kenny to work anymore. But how could he tell his son? He would be so disappointed.

Early the next morning, Kenny got up early, dressed himself, and then sat on his dad's lap while he told him, "Dad, I can't go to work with you today."

His surprised father asked, "Why?"

"Because I will drown in the river," Kenny said.

His father could not stop the tears of joy knowing that Kenny had been warned by the same source he had.[10]

10. David J. Hardy, "Warned in a Dream," *Ensign,* Mar. 1986.

63 *I'll Be Leaving Next Thursday*

What would it be like to know the exact day you were going to die? Barbara Amussen did.

Barbara had been a widow for forty years and had served in the Logan Temple for twenty. One night her husband, Carl, appeared to her in a dream. "It was so real it seemed that he was right in the room. He said he had come to tell me that my time in mortal life was ending and that on the following Thursday (it was then Friday), I would be expected to leave mortal life."

Her oldest daughter, Mabel, said, "Oh, Mother, you've been worrying about something. You've not been feeling well."

"Everything's fine. I feel wonderful. There's nothing to worry about. I just know I'll be leaving next Thursday."

Then she added, "Mabel, when the time comes, I'd like to pass away in your home in the upper room where I used to sit and tell the boys Book of Mormon and Church history stories when they were little fellows."

That Sunday was fast and testimony meeting. She stood and talked as if she were going on a long journey. "She was bidding us all goodbye," her bishop said, "expressing her love for us and the joy that had been hers working in the temple that was just a few yards away from the chapel." She then bore a fervent testimony.

The bishop was so impressed that, following her testimony, he arose and announced the closing song, even though there was still time remaining.

As the days passed, she went to the bank, drew out her small savings, paid all her bills, went to the mortuary, and picked out her casket. She had the water and the power turned off to her home and went to her daughter's. The day before she passed away, her son came to visit. They sat by the bed and held hands as they talked.

On the day of her passing, Mabel came into the room where her mother was reclining on the bed. Her mother said,

"Mabel, I feel a little bit drowsy. I feel I will go to sleep. Do not disturb me if I sleep until the eventide."

Those were her last words, and she slipped peacefully away.[11]

64 *He Dreamed His Daughter's Death*

When Wilford left for his mission to England, his wife Phoebe was expecting a baby. As all missionaries did in those days, he left her in God's keeping, praying for the Lord's blessings to be upon their families in their absence.

Wilford and his companion, George A. Smith, were serving in the city of London, when one night, Wilford dreamed that his wife came to him to tell him that their first child had died.

Wilford believed the dream. The next morning at breakfast, he felt sad. His companion asked him what the matter was; Wilford told him of his dream.

The very next day, a letter arrived from Phoebe telling Wilford of the death of their baby girl. Wilford pondered, "It may be asked what use there was in such a thing [receiving the dream the day before the letter]. I don't know that there was much use in it except to prepare my mind for the news of the death of my child."[12]

MANY ARE LED TO THE GOSPEL THROUGH DREAMS

I have already shared with you the story of the native Americans in Montana who were led to the gospel through sacred dreams. Here are two more stories of individuals who were led to the gospel through sacred dreams. Even more important is the fact that these dreams led to their posterity being blessed with the gospel for generations to come.

11. Ezra Taft Benson, *Come Unto Christ* (Salt Lake City: Deseret Book, 1983), 20–22.
12. *Journal of Discourses*, 26 vols. (London: Latter-day Saints' Book Depot, 1854–86), 22:333–34.

65 He Found the Church in a Dream

John Hillstead was a young man of great faith. He knew that the true gospel of Jesus Christ was somewhere on the earth, and he knew that he had the faith to find it. He continually prayed to be led to the true church.

One Saturday night before going to bed, he knelt and specifically asked the Lord if His church was upon the earth; and if it was, could he find it.

That night, he dreamed he saw a street in the city where he lived. He recognized the street. In a hall on that street, he saw two men preaching the gospel of the Lord Jesus Christ.

He was so impressed by the dream that, when he awoke, he immediately got dressed, went to the street in his dream, found the hall, and heard two Mormon elders preaching the gospel of the Lord Jesus Christ.

At the age of 28, John Hillstead was baptized a member of The Church of Jesus Christ of Latter-day Saints. He and his family later immigrated to Utah from England. His grandson became a General Authority and the Presiding Bishop of the Church, Joseph L. Wirthlin. His great-grandson, Joseph B. Wirthlin, served in the Quorum of the Twelve from 1986–2008.[13]

66 Madeline's Dream

Madeline was only five or six-years-old when she had a remarkable dream concerning her future. She repeated it to her parents, and they noted and remembered it. Her father especially seemed certain that Madeline's dream was not just some whimsical fancy of a young child but would someday come true.

Madeline dreamed that she was sitting in a small strip of meadow close to their vineyard watching to make sure the cows and goats didn't trample or eat the vines. She looked

13. Joseph L. Wirthlin, in Conference Report, April 1952, 116.

up to see three strangers approaching her. At first, she was frightened, but then one of the men spoke and said, "Fear not, for we are the servants of God and have come from afar to preach unto the world the everlasting gospel, which has been restored to the earth in these last days, for the redemption of mankind." A feeling of peace came over her. The messengers told her that God had spoken from the heavens to a young boy and had revealed the everlasting gospel.

To me, the most remarkable part of the dream was that she was told that after her family would receive this new gospel, they would cross the ocean and live in America. Keep in mind that Madeline was only five or six-years-old.

About ten years later, Phillipe Cardon heard news that three men from America were preaching the very things that had been told his daughter in her dream. He "became so excited and so intensely interested that he could not proceed with his work." He left early for home, changed into his best clothes, and went to find the three strangers.

He left Saturday afternoon, traveled a great distance, and arrived Sunday morning in time to hear Elder Lorenzo Snow preach. He invited the men to his home.

When they reached his small mountain home, they found Madeline, now a teenage girl, sitting in a meadow close to the vineyard. She looked up and saw the same three men from her dream ten years earlier. Madeline and her family were soon baptized along with several other families from the area.

In 1854, the Cardon family immigrated to Utah where Madeline married and raised a family of eleven children. She died in 1914 having remained steadfast in the faith she had dreamed of as a child.[14]

14. "Madeline's Dream," *The Friend,* Nov. 1971; see also Elizabeth Maki, "'Suddenly the Thought Came to Me,'" *Church History: Pioneers in Every Land,* June 3, 2013, https://history.lds.org/article/marie-cardon-italy-conversion.

THE LORD USES DREAMS FOR HIS DIVINE PURPOSES

"In all ages and dispensations God has revealed many important instructions and warnings to men by means of dreams."[15] As was mentioned earlier, dreams are *one* of the ways by which God can communicate with us. I believe that some people are given this spiritual gift as some are given the gift of tongues, the gift of healing, or the gift of prophecy, etc.[16]

The way God communicates with us is not important; it is the message that is important. One final story illustrates that Heavenly Father sometimes gives dreams for unusual, but important reasons.

67 *$600 in Gold Pieces*

Peter Nielsen was a convert to The Church of Jesus Christ of Latter-day Saints from Denmark. He had crossed the Atlantic Ocean and then the American plains to join the Saints in "Zion."

He settled his family with many other Danish immigrants in Sanpete County, Utah. There he struggled to make a living and build a home. Just when things looked like he might become a prosperous man, he accepted a call to the Cotton Mission to help settle southern Utah in what would soon be called St. George and Washington.

Again, he struggled to make a living fighting against drought and flooding. He built his family a small, two room, adobe home in Washington and saved as much money as he could to eventually add on to his home and make a fine place for his family to live.

Seven miles away in St. George, a drama was unfolding. The pioneers began building a new tabernacle for the growing community in 1863. Glass for the windows had been ordered from New York and had been shipped around the cape of

15. Parley P. Pratt, *Key to the Science of Theology* (London: Latter-day Saints' Book Depot, 1855), 120.
16. See 1 Corinthians 12:1–11, Moroni 10:8–18 and Doctrine and Covenants 46:8–26.

South America to California. Arrangements had been made to pick up the 2,244 panes in San Bernardino with $800 in cash due at delivery.

David Cannon had been given the assignment to collect the needed money. After painstakingly collecting money from every Latter-day Saint in the area who could give, he had raised $200. How in the world would they find $600 more?

On the night before the teamsters were ready to leave for California to pay for and pick up the glass, he prayed with great faith that somehow the money would come.

The same night David Cannon was praying for money, Peter had a dream that he should give the money he had saved to David Cannon.

He woke early in the morning, and with only the light of a candle to see by, took his savings from his secret hiding place, and told his wife he had to go to St. George. He quickly walked the seven miles and knocked on David Cannon's door. When David answered the door, Peter handed him a red bandana and said, "Good morning, David. I hope I am not too late. You will know what to do with this money."

Peter then turned around and walked the seven miles back to his two room, adobe house, that remained that way for the rest of his life.

When David Cannon emptied the contents of the red bandana onto his table, he counted the gold coins, which added up to exactly $600. Within the hour, the teamsters left for California.[17]

17. Jeffrey R. Holland, "As Doves to Our Windows," *Ensign,* May 2000. Elder Holland cited the source: Andrew Karl Larson, *Red Hills of November* (Salt Lake City: Deseret Book, 1957), 311–13. See also Thomas S. Monson, "Tears, Trials, Trust, Testimony," *Ensign,* May 1987.

Chapter 8

Miracles in Nature

"He is mightier than all the earth."
1 Nephi 4:1

---

68 Mother Nature Was Not Cooperating

The Latter-day Saint elders scheduled a baptismal service on a Tongan beach where five investigators would be baptized; however, Mother Nature was not cooperating. As the group walked down the steep path to the beach, they could see the ocean was at full tide with very heavy waves.

With faith, they began the services. Their singing was drowned out by the crash of the waves. It was now time for the baptisms, but the waves were still monstrous.

One of the missionaries, Elder Carter, stepped into the ocean and commanded it to be still "so these sacred ordinances could be accomplished."

Almost instantly, the ocean calmed. "There were absolutely no more waves."

The baptisms were performed, and the baptismal service concluded. As they began their walk back up the steep path, the ocean waves began crashing in again over the beach.[1]

THE LORD IS IN CONTROL

The first and greatest of all miracles is the creation of this earth and all forms of life placed thereon. This was preceded by the creation of billions of other worlds, and the wonders of our universe continue on into eternity.

Two thousand years ago, the prophet Alma testified to the anti-Christ Korihor: "All things denote there is a God; yea, even the earth, and all things that are upon the face of it, yea, and its motion, yea, and also all the planets which move in their regular form do witness that there is a Supreme Creator" (Alma 30:44).

Could our earth and its place in the universe have all been by chance? I read a fascinating book many years ago titled, *The Evidence of God in an Expanding Universe.*[2] The editor compiled the testimonies of forty prominent scientists concerning their belief in God and the impossibility of this earth coming about by random chance.

One of them, Dr. Irving William Knobloch, of Michigan State University, concluded,

> I believe in God. I believe in Him because I do not think that mere chance could account for the emergence of the first electrons or protons, or the first atoms, or the first amino acids, or for the first protoplasm, or for the first seed, or for the first brain. I believe in God because to me His Divine existence is the only logical explanation for things as they are.[3]

I believe that most, if not all, of the miracles contained in this book are connected to the creation. The great Creator Himself, who organized the elements and formed the foundations of this earth and all things on the face of it, is the same God who walked on water,

---

1. Eric B. Shumway, *Tongan Saints: Legacy of Faith* (Institute for Polynesian Studies, 1991), 84.
2. *The Evidence of God in an Expanding Universe,* Edited by John Clover Monsma (New York: Putnam Publishing, 1958).
3. Ibid., 89.

calmed the seas, and cursed a fig tree to wither and die. If He had that power when He walked the earth, how much more power has He gained as an immortal, resurrected, exalted being? Is there any limit to His power today? Nephi testified to his brothers, "He is mightier than all the earth" (1 Nephi 4:1).

I testify that the Lord Jehovah, creator of the heavens and the earth, is still in control today. The following story is an example: Douglas DeHaan, then President of the Portland Oregon East Stake, was invited to speak at the October 1980 General Conference to tell of the miracle that took place at the church welfare farm in Portland, Oregon.

69 *"Is Anything Too Hard for the Lord?"*

On an island in the Columbia River, the Portland Oregon East Stake developed a dairy farm with about seventy-five acres of land attached that was used to grow corn for silage. October 1, 1977 was scheduled as the harvest date for the corn. Unfortunately, it rained almost every day during the month of September.

President DeHaan knew they were in trouble:

> We have a very high water table on the island, and when the ground gets saturated with too much water we get so much mud our harvest equipment cannot get into the fields without sinking. Once the land is saturated, it takes about a month of dry weather to make the fields passable to vehicles. During the winter months and right up until June, the corn ground is entirely under water.

He drove to the farm on the scheduled harvest date, pulled on his rubber boots, and walked into the fields—thick with mud. There was no way their farm equipment could function. Row after row of ten to fourteen feet high corn would go to waste. His mood was as gloomy as the gray skies.

As he splashed on through mud and water, he was startled to hear a voice. "I am sure that the voice came to me only in my mind, but I could hear the voice and admonition of President Kimball. He said softly, 'Is anything too hard for the Lord?' (Gen. 18:14). . . . I smiled to myself as I walked and said, 'Yes, President, I believe this mess may be too hard even for the Lord.'"

He came to a chopper used to cut the corn. Workers had tried a few days before to harvest the corn with it, but it had sunk past its axles. He climbed up on it and surveyed the seventy-five acres of corn.

> As I looked about in discouragement, the voice seemed to come to me again, but this time in a more serious tone, 'President, is there anything too hard for the Lord?' At once I felt ashamed of my attitude of depression, and soon I was no longer looking down, but up into the sky. Before I realized it, I was talking, yes, pleading aloud with the Lord in faith. When I had finished, I had committed that crop and the harvesting of it into the hands of the Lord and had done so by the power of the priesthood of God.

As he climbed down, tears were streaming down his face. The next day, the sun shone for the first time in nearly thirty days.

On Sunday, President DeHaan attended one of the sacrament meetings held in his stake. He was not scheduled to speak but with ten minutes remaining, the bishop arose and said he felt impressed that their stake president had a spiritual experience he needed to share.

He reluctantly stood yet knew what he had to relate. He asked the congregation to join him with their faith so that their corn could be harvested.

Word rapidly spread throughout the stake. Some members even told their nonmember friends to go ahead and plan outdoor activities because it was not going to rain in October. Every day for the next three weeks the weather forecast called for rain, but each day no rain fell.

About two weeks later, President DeHaan went to Seattle on business. On his flight home, it rained very hard throughout the flight until they reached the Columbia River which surrounded their farm. The clouds parted and the rain ceased.

Three weeks after his experience in the cornfield, President DeHaan drove to the farm. Once again, he put on his boots and walked into the fields. This time the ground was soft but firming—the mud was gone. Plans were made to harvest the corn; many members came to help. They worked day and night for five days. By the following Saturday, all of the freshly chopped corn was safely stored and covered with plastic.

Within an hour, the heavens opened and commenced one of the heaviest and longest downpours anyone could remember. The fields from which the corn had just been removed were flooded and remained under water for the next six months.

President DeHaan stood in the rain with feelings of deep gratitude for the miracle he had witnessed. He knew without a doubt that nothing is too hard for the Lord.[4]

PRIESTHOOD POWER CAN TEMPER THE ELEMENTS

The knowledge that our Creator is still in control today and that God has given that same power to worthy priesthood holders is truly exciting. "We truly can command in the name of Jesus and the very trees obey us, or the mountains, or the waves of the sea" (Jacob 4:6).

Sometimes in the Church you hear the phrase, "temper the elements." Several times in prayers I have heard people implore Heavenly Father to "temper the elements." To temper something means to moderate or control.

Read the following two short stories of righteous men who were able to temper the elements by the authority and power of the holy priesthood they held.

4. Douglas W. DeHaan, "Is Any Thing Too Hard for the Lord?" *Ensign*, Nov. 1980, 87.

70 Command the Winds to Cease

Brigham Young served a mission to England with many of the other apostles from 1839 to 1841. Because of their success, at one point there were more members of The Church of Jesus Christ of Latter-day Saints in England than in the United States.

However, that success had been temporarily halted while they were en route to England. A huge Atlantic storm blocked their path and threatened their very lives.

"I went up on deck and felt impressed in spirit to pray to the Father in the name of Jesus for a forgiveness of my sins. And then I felt to command the winds to cease and let us go safe on our journey," wrote Brigham in his journal.

The storm stopped, and Brigham gave all credit "to that God that rules all things."[5]

71 He Remembered He Held the Holy Priesthood

Franklin D. Richards crossed the Atlantic Ocean many times coming and going to England while in missionary service for the Lord, but on one trip he experienced a storm unlike any he had ever seen. Even the ship's officers were fearful that the waves were rolling so high that the storm would break up the ship.

Suddenly, he remembered he held the holy priesthood which authorized him to act in the Savior's name to control the winds and the waves even as the Savior had done in His ministry.

Elder Richards went to a place in the ship where he could be alone. He raised his hands high towards heaven and, in the name of Jesus Christ, rebuked the storm and commanded the winds and waves to cease their violence and be calm.

The storm immediately subsided.[6]

---

5. Brigham Young, 1837–45 Journal, Nov. 26, 1839. See also D. Michael Quinn, "Brigham Young: Man of the Spirit," *Ensign*, Aug. 1977.
6. Franklin L. West, *Life of Franklin D. Richards* (Salt Lake City: Deseret News Press, 1924), 85–86.

THE POWER OF FAITH AND PRAYER

The prophet Nephi, son of Helaman, through great faith and mighty prayer, persuaded the Lord to place a famine upon his people. The rains immediately ceased, and the wicked Nephites were compelled to humble themselves and repent. Having done so, Nephi again went before the Lord in mighty prayer and pleaded with the Lord to remove the famine. Rain began falling (Helaman 11).

"Faith is a principle of action and of power, and by it one can command the elements."[7]

72 *A Smooth Lane Lay before Us*

When Edward Wood was called as the mission president to Samoa, a General Authority gave him a blessing. He was specifically promised "the elements will be subject to your control. They shall neither destroy you nor retard your travel on land or sea."[8]

That blessing was tested two years later. A conference of the Church was scheduled at the mission headquarters in Apia. President Wood attended meetings on an adjoining island and had planned to leave for the conference with several other natives in time to preside over the conference.

The winds increased, and the sea became rough. It would be extremely dangerous for small boats to cross the fifteen-mile channel.

One of the native Samoans suggested to President Wood that they kneel on the sandy beach and pray. The group sang a hymn and then knelt together as President Wood prayed and "asked the Lord to calm enough of the surface of the ocean so that their boats might cross over the channel in safety."

They launched their boats into the lagoon. As they began to make their way into the ocean, "a smooth lane lay before us all the way across. It was about one hundred feet wide, while on either side the waves were mountainous and the wind very strong."

7. Bible Dictionary, "Faith," 670.
8. The General Authority was Seymour B. Young, Senior President of the Seventy from 1892–1924.

The moment the group set foot at Apia, they knelt on the beach in prayer and thanked God for their deliverance. During the conference, most of those who had witnessed this modern-day miracle bore testimony of the calming of the sea. President Wood's blessing had literally come true.[9]

73 We Cried unto the Lord in Our Afflictions

The Mormon pioneers first arrived in the Salt Lake valley in July of 1847. The small, advanced company was sent to explore and to begin planting crops. Brigham Young had planned for the majority of the Saints to come the next summer giving the advanced company enough time to plant food for all to survive.

Brigham was surprised, indeed angry, when he learned that several wagon trains were headed to the Salt Lake Valley that very fall. How could they all survive?

Conditions during the winter were harsh, and food was scarce. Everyone suffered from lack of food; many survived on roots dug out of the ground.

Spring brought hope as they were able to plant their crops; it looked to be an abundant harvest. Then came the crickets—millions of crickets. The vast horde devoured everything in sight; it looked as if one of the plagues of Moses had descended upon them.

"We cried unto the Lord in our afflictions," said Elder Orson Pratt, "and the Lord heard us, and sent thousands and tens of thousands of a small white bird . . . Many called them gulls, although they were different from the seagulls that live on the Atlantic coast."

The gulls went to work devouring the crickets, and when they had their fill, they would fly back to the lake, vomit them up, and come back for more until the land was cleared of crickets, and their crops were saved.

---

9. *Stories of Insight and Inspiration*, compiled by Margie Calhoun Jensen (Salt Lake City: Bookcraft, 1976), 30–31.

Elder Pratt preached, "There are those who will say that this was one of the natural courses of events, that there was no miracle in it. Let that be as it may, we esteemed it as a blessing from the hand of God; miracle or no miracle, we believe that God had a hand in it, and it does not matter particularly whether strangers believe or not."[10]

Today at Temple Square, you will find a monument on the southwest side of temple dedicated to the gulls that rescued the Saints in their time of need during the summer of 1848.

THE LORD PROVIDES FOR HIS SAINTS

I believe miracles in nature occur around us more often than any of us realize. Sometimes, like in the previous stories, miracles happen because righteous men and women pray in faith or exercise priesthood authority. Sometimes, as in the following stories, God intervenes on our behalf.

74 *"When Dark Clouds of Trouble Hang O'er Us"*

I grew up in Mesa, Arizona where tornados are a rare event, averaging one a year in the entire state. But for some reason, 1972 was a banner year that produced eight tornadoes—one of them near my home.

The date was September 10, 1972, shortly after the beginning of my junior year at Mesa High School. Late in the afternoon, thick dark clouds moved in from the east. From inside the chapel, the noise of the storm was so strong that at times it overshadowed the speaker. When hail began pelting the roof, the speaker actually stopped speaking because he couldn't be heard.

Suddenly, it became quiet and the speaker continued. Then just as suddenly, the noise became a roar. The power went out, and the congregation was thrust into darkness.

10. *Journal of Discourses*, 26 vols. (London: Latter-day Saints' Book Depot, 1854–86), 21:278.

Unbeknownst to the congregation, a tornado had touched down only a few blocks away from the church and had moved in their direction.

About 500 members of the church were sitting in the chapel with the fury of the storm raging over them. No one had a clue how serious the situation was outside.

Inside the chapel, the members felt calm; everyone was quiet as they listened to the mighty power of nature. From the back of the chapel, someone began to sing, "We Thank Thee, O God, For a Prophet." Soon the entire congregation had joined in. When the second verse began, some members could not hold back the tears: "When dark clouds of trouble hang o'er us and threaten our peace to destroy, there is hope smiling brightly before us, and we know that deliverance is nigh."[11]

The storm gradually died, and the meeting was concluded; the last 45 minutes had been in total darkness.

No one was prepared for what they saw as they left the chapel—utter destruction everywhere. The storm had downed power lines and trees, had ripped the roofs off of houses, had broken windows, had filled the curbs and gutters with hail, and had flooded the streets. Later, I learned that the tornado had caused $1,000,000 in damage.

Miraculously, not one home of those who had been in church sustained any serious damage.

What had happened to the chapel where 500 members had met during the tornado? If you could have seen it from the air, you would have seen a church building smack dab in the middle of the destruction, yet the storm had not damaged any shingles, or broken any windows. It was as if a protective shield had been placed over the entire chapel.[12]

In spite of incredible damage to the area, the Lord had protected His Saints.

---

11. "We Thank Thee, O God, For a Prophet," *Hymns,* 19.
12. Joyce A. Organ, "Tornado!" *Ensign*, Feb. 1973, 37–39.

75 *The Miracle of the Quail*

Brigham Young and the majority of the Saints had been forced from Nauvoo, Illinois in February 1846. About seven miles west of the Mississippi river, President Young established a temporary staging area for the exodus across Iowa. They called it Sugar Creek. Future Latter-day Saint refugees also used Sugar Creek on their way west.

By September 1846, most members of the Church had left Nauvoo; only the most severely ill and those totally destitute were left. That wasn't good enough for the enemies of the Church, however. The mob wanted *all* the Mormons gone from Nauvoo. What became known as "The Battle of Nauvoo" ensued, resulting in the expulsion of 640 more Saints.

They were ill-equipped for the journey. As they crossed the mighty Mississippi River, and straggled into Sugar Creek, it was obvious why they became known as the "poor camp."

On October 9, 1846, Thomas Bullock recorded the following in his journal: "This morning we had a direct manifestation of the mercy and goodness of God, in a miracle being performed in the camp."

Several large flocks of quail flew into the camp, some landing on their breakfast tables; even children could easily catch the birds alive in their hands. "Men who were not in the church marveled at the sight—the brethren and sisters praised God and glorified His name, that what was showered down upon the children of Israel in the wilderness is manifested unto us in our persecution. . . . Every man, woman, and child had quail to eat for dinner."[13]

13. *Thomas Bullock Diary*, 9 Oct. 1846, LDS Historical Department, Salt Lake City, Utah.

Chapter 9

Healing Physical Infirmities

"Have ye any that are lame, or blind, or maimed,
or that are withered, or that are deaf?
Bring them hither and I will heal them."
3 Nephi 17:7

---

76 *I Did Not Feel Any More Pain*

Margarete Hellmann suffered from a hip ailment since childhood. The pain increased year by year until she was forced to walk with crutches. She felt pain with every step. Members of her ward contributed money to buy a wheelchair for her, but soon, she found even sitting in a chair brought unbearable pain. To make matters worse, she developed inflammation of the nerves on the left side of her face.

One day, she heard that the prophet of the Lord, Spencer W. Kimball, was coming to East Germany for a conference. She thought of the story in the New Testament of the woman who had been afflicted for twelve long years and had been healed by only touching the hem of the Savior's clothes. He had lovingly said to her, "Daughter, thy faith hath made thee whole; go in peace, and be whole" (Mark 5:25–34).

Margarete determined that she could be like that woman. She desired more than anything else in her heart to touch the prophet when he came to Dresden. She had complete faith that he would not even have to take time to lay his hands on her head and give her a blessing—if she could just touch him.

Over 1,200 people packed the meeting place; it looked as if not one more person could be squeezed in. Some Latter-day Saints had traveled hundreds of miles to be there.

Sister Hellmann's grandson, Frank, brought her to the service early to position her wheelchair near the aisle where the prophet was to pass. There was scarcely a dry eye in the congregation as President Kimball spoke.

Margarete later told the rest of the story: "When our prophet came close to me, he warmly shook my hand and looked at me in the spirit of love, as did those who were with him. After that, I did not feel any more pain—not then, nor any to this day. That is the greatest testimony of my life!"[1]

WE LIVE IN A FALLEN WORLD

We live in an imperfect world. As beautiful as it is, our world is beset with wars, famines, disease, and death. Even our physical bodies created in the image of God have numerous defects and deficiencies. Does that mean God is not perfect? Absolutely not! It means that, since the fall of Adam and Eve, man has lived in a fallen world that brought natural and varying consequences.

The scriptures often speak of infirmities. An infirmity is a physical or mental weakness. The apostle Paul called his infirmity a "thorn in the flesh" (2 Corinthians 12:7-10). Rather than thinking that God was punishing him, Paul felt his infirmity was to keep him humble and that, through Christ, his weakness was made strong.

The prophet Isaiah prophesied of the time when a future Messiah would bless those who had infirmities: "Then the eyes of the blind shall be opened, and the ears of the deaf shall be unstopped. Then

1. Joseph B. Wirthlin, "Let Your Light So Shine," *Ensign*, Nov. 1978, 36.

shall the lame man leap . . . and the tongue of the dumb sing" (Isaiah 35:5–6).

The New Testament and the Book of Mormon are filled with examples of Jesus having mercy upon those with infirmities—both physical and mental. Some He healed, and some He did not, but He had compassion on all.

There is only one example of Jesus healing a deaf person. In the Gospel of Mark, Jesus was asked *publicly* to heal the man, but He only performed the miracle after He took the man aside *privately.* "And he took him aside from the multitude, and put his fingers into his ears . . . and looking up to heaven, he sighed, and saith unto him, Ephphatha, that is, Be opened" (Mark 7:33–34).

Could Jesus open the ears of the deaf today?

77 *I Heard the Blessing*

A group of Latter-day Saint teenagers in Arizona befriended a deaf young woman who was not a member of The Church of Jesus Christ of Latter-day Saints. Their kindness gave her a desire to take the missionary lessons. With the permission of her parents, she did so and was soon scheduled for baptism.

After one of the missionaries baptized her and she had changed into dry clothing, she was confirmed a member of the Church and given the gift of the Holy Ghost. The elder who confirmed her pronounced a beautiful blessing.

Her new Bishop, Burke Peterson, was uneasy at first at the incredible things she was promised, but then felt a spirit of peace come over him. He thought to himself, "If only she could *see* the elder, she could hear this wonderful blessing." He listened carefully, so he could invite her into his office after the blessing where she could see him talk and tell her what had been said. I once had a deaf woman attend my Sunday school class. With astonishment, I saw that she understood almost every word I spoke, she only had to watch my mouth move.

Bishop Peterson invited her into his office and sat in front of her. "I want to tell you of the blessing the elder gave you. It was tremendous."

With tears in her eyes, the young woman stopped him and said, "Bishop, I *heard* the blessing."

She was healed and her hearing was fully restored.[2]

IN THE NAME OF JESUS

I have always loved the story of Peter and John in the temple healing a man who had never walked. With power, Peter looked on the beggar and said, "Silver and gold have I none; but such as I have give I thee: In the name of Jesus Christ of Nazareth rise up and walk" (Acts 3:1–6). The story is a perfect example of a priesthood holder invoking the Savior's name to bless someone with a physical infirmity.

Modern day miracles cannot be performed under our own power. Although the name of Jesus is not always spoken, be certain that miracles are only done by His power.

78 *He Will Bless Me, and I Will Walk*

Most children have remarkable faith. A six-year-old boy in Brazil heard that an apostle was coming to speak at a conference of the Church near his home. He told the elders, "When the apostle comes, he will bless me, and I will walk." The boy had never walked, but he had faith he would someday.

The apostle Harold B. Lee toured the missions of the Church in Central and South America in 1959. When he arrived in Brazil, a missionary asked Elder Lee, "Would you be kind enough to join with us in blessing this little boy?"

Elder Lee went with the elders; the father carried the boy and sat him in a chair. Overcome with emotion, the boy cried throughout the blessing.

When Elder Lee arrived back home to the United States, he was shown a picture of the little boy standing on his feet for the first time. A miraculous healing had occurred.

While President of the Church, Harold B. Lee told this story and then said, "That miracle didn't come because of me; it didn't come because of the elders; this was because the

---

2. H. Burke Peterson, "The Ministry of the Aaronic Priesthood Holder," *Ensign*, Oct. 1981.

Lord himself, by my hand and the hands of the elders, put his hands upon the head of that little boy by our hands and he received the strength . . . to stand on his feet for the first time since birth."[3]

79 *The Healing of John Tanner's Leg*

Poor John Tanner had been troubled for many years with sores on his leg—like that of a fever sore. His leg finally became so bad that he could no longer walk on it; for five months he had put no weight on his bad leg. The doctors said it must be amputated to save his life. John said, "No!" He and his leg would go together. He began to put his affairs in order.

It was then that John heard rumors of a strange people called "Mormons." They were supposedly "going about turning the world upside down." They were scheduled to preach about seven miles from his home, and so John went to the meeting to save others from being duped. His foot was bolstered up as high as his seat to keep the swelling down.

When he heard the missionaries from The Church of Jesus Christ of Latter-day Saints, he knew he had heard the truth. He told his Baptist friends that they had better not fight against it, "lest they unhappily find themselves fighting against God."

The two missionaries, Simeon and Jared Carter, told John that if he would read the Book of Mormon and believed it, "he should see an alteration in his leg." John bought a Book of Mormon and took it home. He read it over and over again while comparing it with the Bible. He believed it and set his bad foot on the ground for the first time in five months.

The missionaries soon came to see him. Elder Jared Carter asked him if he would be afraid to put his foot down if he commanded him in the name of the Lord to rise and walk.

John did not reply. Elder Carter said, while placing his hand on his shoulder, "In the name of Jesus Christ I command you to arise and walk."

3. "Speaking for Himself—President Lee's Stories," *Ensign*, Feb. 1974, 19–20.

John Tanner rose to his feet. Elder Carter encouraged him: "You need not be afraid to put down your foot. Remember, you do it in the name of the Lord." John laid aside his crutch and walked back and forth from the front porch through a long hall and into a long kitchen. He wept and praised God "for His mercy in bringing the Gospel and its attending blessings."

The next day, John, his wife, and son Nathan were baptized. He remained a faithful member of the Church for the remainder of his life.[4]

80 *I Command Thee to Be Whole*

One of my favorite stories from Church History is the healing of Elsa Johnson. Elsa and her husband, John, lived in Hiram, Ohio, about thirty miles south of Kirtland. She had been afflicted with rheumatism—unable to raise her arm and hand for two years.

The Johnson's heard about the "Mormons," and they greatly desired to meet the Prophet Joseph Smith. They traveled to Kirtland and took with them their minister, Ezra Booth.

While they were visiting with Joseph, the subject of spiritual gifts came up, the kind that was known during the days of the Savior and His apostles. Someone in the room said, "Here is Mrs. Johnson with a lame arm; has God given any power now on the earth to cure her?"

A few moments later when the conversation had turned in another direction, Joseph Smith arose, walked over to Mrs. Johnson, took her by the hand, and in a solemn manner said: "Woman, in the name of the Lord Jesus Christ, I command thee to be whole."

Joseph immediately left the room. Those remaining were "awe-stricken at the infinite presumption of the man, and the calm assurance with which he spoke."

---

4. *Writings of Early Latter-day Saints and Their Contemporaries,* A Database Collection. Excerpts edited by Milton Backman and Keith Perkins, 2nd ed., rev. (Provo, Utah: Religious Studies Center, 1996), 52.
See also Nathan Tanner, "Incidents in the Life of Nathan Tanner," *Descendants of Nathan Tanner (Sr.),* (Nathan Tanner Association, 1942), 51–61.

Suddenly, Elsa Johnson lifted her previously afflicted arm with ease. The next day she returned home and did the family's wash without difficulty or pain for the first time in years.

Ezra Booth, the minister who accompanied the Johnsons and witnessed the miracle, joined the new church. However, as in a previously mentioned story, the miracle may have convinced him, but it did not convert him. Ezra Booth wanted the same power Joseph had—he wanted to perform miracles. When he found that this was not the way the Lord worked, he turned away from the true gospel and became an apostate.[5]

SPIRITUAL GIFTS: THE FAITH TO HEAL AND THE FAITH TO BE HEALED

"Spiritual gifts are blessings or abilities given by God to His children through the power of the Holy Ghost. Gifts of the Spirit are given to bless and benefit those who love the Lord and seek to keep His commandments."[6]

The scriptures list several spiritual gifts, including: knowledge, wisdom, faith, prophecy, speaking in tongues, and interpretation of tongues.[7] Several modern-day apostles have spoken of spiritual gifts not listed in the scriptures, such as the gift to ponder and the gift to be calm.[8] Elder Bruce R. McConkie said that, "Spiritual gifts are endless in number and infinite in variety."[9]

Two spiritual gifts pertain specifically to this chapter: "to some it is given to have faith to be healed; and to others it is given to have faith to heal" (Doctrine and Covenants 46:19–20).

Did you catch the subtle difference? Some priesthood holders have such great faith that they *know* that when they bless an afflicted soul,

5. Joseph Smith, *History of The Church of Jesus Christ of Latter-day Saints,* Edited by B. H. Roberts. 2nd ed. rev., 7 vols. (Salt Lake City: The Church of Jesus Christ of Latter-day Saints, 1932–51), 1:215–216. Elsa Johnson's miracle is recorded in the History of Ohio.
6. "Spiritual Gifts," *Gospel Topics,* churchofjesuschrist.org/study/manual/gospel-topics/spiritual-gifts.
7. See 1 Corinthians 12:1–11, Moroni 10:17–25, and Doctrine and Covenants 46:8–26.
8. Robert D. Hales, "Gifts of the Spirit," Brigham Young University Fireside, Aug. 1, 1993, speeches.byu.edu.
9. Bruce R. McConkie, *A New Witness for the Articles of Faith* (Salt Lake City: Deseret Book, 2007), 371.

the Lord working through them will cause that person to be healed. Such is the case with President Heber C. Kimball in the second of the two stories that follow.

Both stories that follow show the power of someone who has faith to *be* healed. These stories are modern day examples of the apostle Peter healing a lame man because, "he had faith to be healed" (Acts 14:8–10).

81 *He Raised the Bandage Slightly*

John Ruothoff had to drop out of school—he could no longer see. He was only eleven-years old. John's eyes had given him problems for many years, and his sight had slowly diminished.

He was a faithful member of The Church of Jesus Christ of Latter-day Saints in Holland. One day, it was announced in church that the president of the Church was coming to Rotterdam, Holland—the very city where he lived.

John said to his mother, "The prophet has the most power of any missionary on earth. If you will take me with you to the meeting, and he will look into my eyes, I believe they will be healed."

When I first heard this story, I was struck by the fact that John didn't even feel like he needed to have the prophet lay his hands on his head to give him a priesthood blessing; he had the faith that if the prophet would just look into his eyes, he would be healed.

According to his desire, John went to the conference with his mother. At the close of the meeting, President Joseph F. Smith walked down the aisle and shook hands with members of the congregation. John's mother led her son with his bandaged eyes towards the prophet.

President Smith took him by the hand and spoke to him kindly. He then raised the bandages from John's eyes and looked into them sympathetically, saying something in English which John did not understand.

When John and his mother arrived home, he took off his bandages and then cried out to his mother, "Mama, my eyes are well; I cannot feel any more pain. I can see now, and far too."[10]

82 Open Your Eyes, Brother William

William Moroni Palmer was a very happy, playful, normal little boy until the age of five. As his family traveled by wagon train to Utah, an epidemic of acute conjunctivitis (pink eye) broke out in the camp. William contracted the inflammation.

Someone in the camp who had done some "doctoring" bathed his eyes in a solution which made him completely blind.

The family continued on to the Salt Lake valley and later settled in Ogden, about sixty miles north.

William's mother spent many hours reading to him. He especially loved Bible stories and would memorize them until he could quote them word for word. His faith in the Lord grew.

One day, after seven years of blindness, he heard his family talking about President Heber C. Kimball, a counselor in the First Presidency. He was coming to Ogden for a conference of the Church.

Later that day, when William was alone with his mother, he said to her, "Mother, would you ask Brother Heber C. Kimball to come to our place after the conference, and bless me so that I can see?" In those days, only the adults went to conference.

Patience Palmer took her not-so-small-now twelve-year-old son into her arms and said, "Dear William, do you believe you can be healed?"

"I know I can, Momma, if he will come."

On the day of the conference, the family knelt in prayer. After his parents left, William spent most of the time praying alone in his mother's room.

William's keen ears were the first to hear the horse and buggy drive down the lane to their home. He listened intently

10. Joseph Fielding Smith, *Life of Joseph F. Smith* (Salt Lake City: Deseret Book, 1969), 397.

and heard the sound he had been waiting for—the voice of President Kimball.

"Is this the boy you told me of?" President Kimball said as he entered the house and saw the eager face of the young man.

"It is," Patience said, "but would you like to eat with us first?"

"*This* must come first. He has waited long enough."

Abraham Palmer placed a chair in the center of the room. He anointed his son with consecrated oil, and then he and President Heber C. Kimball laid their hands on William's head. President Kimball sealed the anointing and then pronounced a blessing.

He then said, "Open your eyes, Brother William, and you shall see."

William's eyes flew open. He sat stunned for a moment, and then he leaped out of his chair, across the room, and out the door crying, "Oh! I can see! I can see! Oh, Momma, I can see!" William fell to the grass and hugged the earth.[11]

---

11. Ronda Gibb Hinrichsen, "William's Faith," *The Friend*, April 1998, 44–45. I first discovered this delightful story in the Friend magazine. I learned later that it was taken from "A Brief History of the Life of William Moroni Palmer," written by his son and daughter, Asael E. Palmer and Ada A. Palmer Orgill. His eyesight was not perfect, but William had good near-sighted vision. When reading, he would hold the book about six inches from his face and could read for hours without tiring.

Chapter 10

Power Over Death

"Why should it be thought a thing incredible with you, that God should raise the dead?"
Acts 26:8

---

83 *Send for the Elders; I Don't Feel Very Well*

Elder Matthew Cowley of the Council of the Twelve Apostles related the following story that took place while he served as the mission president in New Zealand.

Elder Cowley was called to the home of a member of the Church who had died; his body was being prepared for burial. Elder Cowley had not been there long when the dead man's brother ran in.

"Administer to him," the brother said.

Someone said, "Why, you shouldn't do that; he's dead."

The brother demanded, "You do it!"

A young man holding the Melchizedek priesthood got down on his knees and anointed the dead man with consecrated oil. His brother then blessed him and commanded him to rise.

The dead man sat up and said, "Send for the elders; I don't feel very well."

They told him that he had just been administered to, and he said, "Oh, that was it. I was dead. I could feel life coming back unto me just like a blanket unrolling."

He outlived the brother who blessed him.[1]

GOD HAS POWER OVER DEATH

The apostle Paul told the Corinthian Saints, "The last enemy that shall be destroyed is death" (1 Corinthians 15:26). The ultimate fulfillment of that prophecy will be at the end of the Millennium when those who inhabited the earth will be resurrected and receive a perfect body of flesh and bones.[2]

The greatest of all miracles to have ever transpired on this earth, since its creation, is the resurrection of Jesus the Christ, the Son of God. But no less miraculous is the reality that every living creature who lived and died while on this earth will also be resurrected. The prophet Isaiah prophesied of the coming Messiah when he said, "He will swallow up death in victory; and the Lord God will wipe away tears from off all faces" (Isaiah 25:8).

In a few, rare instances, people who have died have been brought back to life—not in a resurrected state but returned to their mortal body—to later face another date with death and eventually resurrection.

The first recorded scriptural example of someone being raised from the dead took place nearly eight hundred years before Christ raised Lazarus from his tomb. The prophet Elijah had been commanded to go to a small village named Zarephath located on the shores of the Mediterranean Sea, in what is now Lebanon. There he was shown the utmost hospitality from a widow who had very little food to share. By the power of the priesthood, Elijah performed a miracle on her behalf so that her barrel of meal and her container of oil continued to be replenished. He then performed a second miracle on her behalf bringing her dead son back to life (1 Kings 17:17–24).

1. Matthew Cowley, "Miracles," Brigham Young University devotional, Feb. 18, 1953, speeches.byu.edu.
2. See Alma 11:42–44. Exceptions will be those few called sons of perdition—see Doctrine and Covenants 76:30–49.

During the Savior's mortal ministry, He raised at least four people from the dead. Bringing back Lazarus after being dead for three days was seen as the ultimate proof that Jesus truly was the promised Messiah.[3]

The scriptures also record the apostles of Jesus performing the same kind of miracles: Paul raised Eutychus (Acts 20:7–12); Peter raised Tabitha (Acts 9:36–43); Nephi brought back his brother Timothy from the dead (3 Nephi 7:18–20).[4]

Could the dead be brought back to life in our day?

84 I Never Felt Better in My Life

William Huntington was born in 1818. He died the *second* time in 1887; his body is located in Utah in the historic Springville cemetery. The account of his *first* death in 1839 witnesses to the power and authority given to the Prophet Joseph Smith.

William was baptized a member of The Church of Jesus Christ of Latter-day Saints in 1836 at the age of seventeen. He moved with his parents to be with the Saints in Missouri and was then driven from the state by powerful mobs. The family settled in Commerce, Illinois which was soon renamed Nauvoo.

Before it was drained, Nauvoo was a swamp infested by malaria-carrying mosquitos. Although young and healthy, William Huntington did not escape the plague. At the time, he was living with and working for Joseph Smith and his family.

William was afflicted for weeks and grew weaker day by day. Toward the end, he could not move or speak. Friends and family came to his bedside to mourn his passing.

"Observing his situation [William] found that he was in the upper part of the room near the ceiling, and could see the body he had occupied lying on the bed, with weeping friends, standing around . . ."

---

3. John 11:1–44. The other three recorded accounts are in Matthew 9:18–16, Luke 7:11–17 and 3 Nephi 26:15.
4. 4 Nephi 1:5 alludes to the apostles raising others from the dead.

While standing near the ceiling, "he saw Joseph Smith and two other brethren come into the room. Joseph turned to his wife Emma and asked her to get him a dish of clean water."

After washing their hands, Joseph and those with him "stepped to the bed and laid their hands upon the head of his body, which at that time looked loathsome to him, and as the three stretched out their hands . . . he by some means became aware that he must go back into that body, and started to do so."

As Joseph said "amen," William again felt his physical body. "The feeling for a moment was most excruciating, as though his body was pierced in every part with some sharp instruments." He sat up in bed and put his feet on the floor. Joseph told him to be careful because he was still weak.

William replied, "I never felt better in my life. I want my pants."

He sat in a chair near the bed and asked for some bread and milk; he relished every bite. Everyone in the room was astonished. A few minutes before they had wept in sorrow; now they wanted to weep for joy.

Joseph Smith declared "they had just witnessed as great a miracle as Jesus did while on the earth. They had seen the dead brought to life."

A few months later, William married. Joseph appointed him as a constable in Nauvoo, and as the city sexton. A sexton cares for the cemetery and keeps careful records of those buried there. Ironically, the first death he listed was that of Zina Huntington, his mother.

William traveled with the Saints west and settled in Springville, Utah. After sharing this sacred experience with a friend, he testified: "Now I have told you the truth, and here I am a live man, sitting by the side of you on this log, and I testify that Joseph Smith was a Prophet of God."[5]

---

5. Levi Curtis, "Recollections of the Prophet Joseph Smith," Juvenile Instructor 27, no. 12, 15 June 1892, 385–86. See also Dennis Home, *Faith to Heal and to be Healed: Insights drawn from inspirational accounts* (Springville, UT: Cedar Fort Inc., 2009), 102.

85 *He Called Me Back*

The following story occurred in 1891 when Lorenzo Snow was President of the Quorum of the Twelve Apostles. It fulfills the prophecy made in his patriarchal blessing: "the dead shall rise and come forth at thy bidding."

Seventeen-year-old Ella Jensen hovered between life and death with scarlet fever for weeks at her home in Brigham City, Utah. Her friend, Leah, came one evening to stay with her and relieve Ella's parents. Ella seemed to be getting worse and could only talk in a whisper.

Early the next morning, Leah was awakened by Ella calling her name. "I hurried to her bed. She was all excited and asked me to get the comb, brush, and scissors, explaining that she wanted to brush her hair and trim her fingernails and get all ready."

Ella told her friend, "They are coming to get me at ten o'clock in the morning."

"Who is coming?"

"Uncle Hans Jensen and the messengers. I am going to die and they are coming at ten o'clock to get me and take me away."

Leah tried unsuccessfully to get Ella to go back to sleep. Her parents were summoned, and Ella again related the vision as she had received it. Throughout the morning, she continued to decline. Leah left at 8:00 a.m., but Ella's father and mother continued at her bedside.

About 10:00 a.m., Jake Jensen was holding his daughter's hand when he could feel her pulse weaken. A few minutes later, he turned to his wife and said, "Althea, she is dead; her pulse has stopped."

It was Sunday morning, and stake conference had just begun in the new Box Elder Tabernacle in Brigham City. President Lorenzo Snow was speaking. Jake Jensen decided to go into town and give President Snow a message, so he could announce the death of Ella to the congregation.

When President Snow received the note, he paused to read it and then excused himself, telling the congregation nothing of Ella's death, only that he needed to leave to visit a family in deep sorrow. He took with him the Box Elder Stake President, Rudger Clawson.

When they arrived, Presidents Snow and Clawson stood for a moment at Ella's bedside. They could feel that her spirit had left her body and passed through the veil. President Snow then turned to Jake Jensen and asked if he had any consecrated oil in the home. Brother Jensen was surprised at this request but went to retrieve it.

President Snow then turned to Rudger Clawson and said, "Brother Clawson, will you anoint her?" He did.

Lorenzo Snow then also laid his hands on the seventeen-year-old girl and said, "Dear Ella, I command you in the name of the Lord, Jesus Christ to come back and live, your mission is not ended."

President Snow then turned to the overwhelmed parents and said, "Now do not mourn or grieve anymore. It will be all right. Brother Clawson and I are busy and must go; we cannot stay, but you just be patient and wait." They left.

Jake and Althea Jensen looked back at their daughter on the bed—she did not move.

They waited by her bedside. News of Ella's death quickly spread throughout the small town and friends came to offer condolences.

For more than an hour, they sat by her bedside trying to have faith in President Snow's promise. All at once, she opened her eyes.

She looked at her parents and then around the room as if looking for someone. "Where is he?" she said.

"Where is who?"

"Why Brother Snow," she replied. "He called me back."

Brother and Sister Jensen explained to their daughter that he had left. Ella's head dropped back to the pillow and she said, "Why did he call me back? I was so happy and did not want to come back." She then related her remarkable experiences in the spirit world during the more than three hours she had been gone.

Ella Jensen Wight lived to become the mother of eight children. In fact, she outlived all the other participants in this great drama.[6]

RIGHTEOUS BEARERS OF THE MELCHIZEDEK PRIESTHOOD HAVE THE POWER TO RAISE THE DEAD

The Prophet Joseph Smith was once asked if Mormons could raise the dead. He replied, "No, but God can raise the dead, through man as an instrument."[7]

The five modern-day examples used in this chapter were all performed by righteous Melchizedek Priesthood holders. These stories are witnesses that every type of miracle performed by Jesus and His apostles can be done today.

Even a newly ordained eighteen-year-old elder has the authority to raise the dead.

86 *I Can't Get a Pulse!*

It was a Wednesday afternoon in late September. A. J. Edwards and his Little League football teammates had just completed warm-ups. The skies were darkening, and it looked like rain. Suddenly, a powerful bolt of lightning struck the field accompanied by a simultaneous, deafening clap of thunder.

The entire team felt the impact; some were knocked to the ground and most were dazed. The boys and coaches started running for shelter; some began to cry or fell to their knees and prayed. A. J. Edwards did not move—he had taken a direct hit.

The coaches suddenly saw A. J.'s condition and ran to his side.

6. LeRoi C. Snow, "Raised from the Dead," *Improvement Era,* Sept. 1929, 881–86, 972–80. Also quoted in Leon R. Hartshorn, comp., *Classic Stories from the Lives of Our Prophets* (Salt Lake City: Deseret Book, 1971), 145–48.
7. Joseph Smith, *Teachings of the Prophet Joseph Smith*, Selected by Joseph Fielding Smith (Salt Lake City: Deseret Book, 1976), 120.

"I can't get a pulse," said David Johnson, "He's in cardiac arrest."

David and another coach began CPR.

Eighteen-year-old Bryce Reynolds cradled A. J.'s head in his hands as the other men feverishly worked to save his life. Bryce was the young defensive coach for the team.

As he watched the life-against-death struggle, Bryce had an impression. He remembered vividly a priesthood blessing that the bishop had once given his grandfather following an accident years earlier. Now, as he held this young boy in his arms, he realized that for the first time in his life he needed to use his newly conferred Melchizedek Priesthood. Bryce had been ordained an elder less than six weeks earlier.

Bryce said, "A. J. Edwards, in the name of the Lord Jesus Christ and by the power and authority of the Melchizedek Priesthood which I hold, I bless you that you will be OK. In the name of Jesus Christ, amen."

A. J. Edwards immediately started breathing again.

More blessings and miracles would follow in the weeks to come. A. J. Edwards is now healthy, has served a full-time mission for The Church of Jesus Christ of Latter-day Saints, and is indeed okay.[8]

THEY ONLY ACTED AFTER BEING PROMPTED BY THE SPIRIT

I purposely placed this type of miracle toward the end of this book—they are rare. Death has a purpose, and our Heavenly Father wants us to return to Him. So, when someone, even a righteous Melchizedek Priesthood holder calls someone back from the dead, he must only do so after being divinely inspired by the Holy Ghost.

If it is God's will that someone who has died should live again, he will make his will known to someone who is worthy to use His priesthood authority to act in the name of God and who has developed the ability to listen to the promptings of the Holy Ghost.

8. Jeffrey R. Holland, "Sanctify Yourselves," *Ensign*, Nov. 2000, 50–51.

The next example shows a righteous man seeking to know the will of God, but when he acted he was told to wait until the right moment. Sometimes, miracles are so sacred that they must only be done in private, away from the unbelieving of heart.

87 *She Will Return to You Tomorrow*

Tisina was run over by a taxi full of American soldiers. It was not their fault. The three-year-old girl had run out into the street near her home. Thousands of soldiers from the United States had been stationed in Tonga during the second World War. Tisina slipped away from the other children walking at the side of the road. She was so small that the soldiers in the vehicle never even knew they had struck the girl until a villager yelled at them to stop.

The soldiers carried Tisina's lifeless body to her home. Her father opened the door and saw four foreigners holding the mangled body of his daughter, her skull crushed, and her face disfigured. It was a traumatic moment for everyone involved. The soldiers felt awful, but the villagers testified to the family that it had not been their fault.

One of the soldiers spoke to the heartbroken father and offered to take his daughter to the hospital to repair the damages done to her face.

"Will the repair bring her back to life?" he said.

The American sadly admitted, "No, but the doctors can fix up her head and face for the funeral."

The father, Iohani Wolfgramm, said he did not want them to take her away. He asked the soldiers to carry her body into the chapel next door to their home. Iohani would pray to God as to what he should do.

While the soldiers held Tisina, Iohani laid his hands on her head to give her a priesthood blessing. By then, several curious villagers had joined the solemn scene. Iohani could not speak. His tongued felt tied. He received the strong impression, "This is not the right time, for the place is full of mockers and unbelievers. Wait for a private moment."

Iohani removed his hands from his daughter's head and said to those gathered, "The Lord has restrained me from blessing this little girl, because there are unbelievers among you who doubt this sacred ordinance. Please help me by leaving so I can bless my child."

The people slowly and respectfully left. Tisina was placed in a bed and covered with a sheet. Iohani waited for three hours.

By this time, his wife, Salote, was beside herself. "Why are you waiting to do something? When are you going to bless her? Her body is beginning to harden. Isn't it better to prepare her for burial while her body is still soft and warm?"

Iohani told his wife that the Spirit had restrained him from giving the blessing. Meanwhile, curious villagers continued to come to inquire about Tisina.

About 8:00 p.m., Iohani received a strong impression that now was the time to bless the child. "The feeling of what I should do and say was so strong within me that I knew Tisina would recover completely after the blessing."

He anointed her head with consecrated oil and then blessed her in the name of Jesus Christ "to be well and normal." During the blessing he asked God "to open the doors of Paradise, so I could tell her to come back and receive her body again and live."

Then came the test of faith. When the "Amen" was pronounced, she did not move or open her eyes—Tisina was still dead.

Two hours later, Salote asked her husband if they should start preparing the body for the funeral. Iohani said, "Go to sleep. She will come back to us tomorrow. The Lord has told me."

At 3:00 a.m., Iohani felt a tiny hand pulling his hair. He awoke to find Tisina alive and well. He grabbed her and examined her head and face. She was completely healed.[9]

9. Eric B. Shumway, *Tongan Saints: Legacy of Faith* (Institute for Polynesian Studies, 1991), 87–89.

THOSE BROUGHT BACK HAD A MISSION TO FULFILL

I mentioned earlier in the chapter that Jesus and His apostles had raised several individuals from the dead. These were not resurrections but restorations to life. Jesus would be the first to be resurrected. These individuals were called back to continue their mortal sojourn until they died again and then awaited the day of their resurrection in the spirit world.

Jesus purposely waited until Lazarus had been dead for over three days to bring him back. The Jews believed that a person's spirit remained close to his body for up to three days.[10] The people could no longer deny that Jesus was the promised Messiah. He had the power to raise the dead.

Lazarus's purpose in returning from the dead then was three-fold: (1) he was one of the means by which the Savior testified that He was Jehovah; (2) the raising of Lazarus was also a foreshadowing of the resurrection of Jesus; (3) Lazarus became a living witness that Jesus was the Christ. The Jews even tried to have him killed in order to get rid of the evidence (John 12:9–11).

Each of us has a mission to perform on this earth. For some, the mission is brief—to obtain a physical body. Others have missions to be inventors, musicians, great leaders, etc. When our life is cut shorter than what we or our loved ones expect, there is sadness and grief. In the case of seventeen-year-old Ella Jensen, she was called back by an apostle to finish her mission and to become the mother of eight children.

The following stories illustrate two people who died, went to the spirit world, and then returned to their bodies to fulfil a specific mission. In the first story, Phoebe was given a choice to return to her mortal body if she agreed to certain conditions. In the second story, Don requested to return for a short time to comfort his family.

---

10. Bruce R. McConkie, D*octrinal New Testament Commentary*, 3 vols. (Salt Lake City: Bookcraft, 1965–73), 1:533.

88 *Yes, I Will Do It*

Wilford's wife, Phoebe, was dying. He did his best to care for her but one evening her spirit slipped away. The women helping to care for her wept. Wilford could only stare in sorrow.

"The spirit and power of God began to rest upon me," he recalled, "until for the first time during her sickness, faith filled my soul although she lay before me as one dead."

Wilford retrieved his consecrated oil, bowed his head, and prayed for the life of his dear Phoebe. He then anointed her, laid his hands upon her, and rebuked the power of death in the name of Jesus Christ. He commanded the destroyer to depart from her "and the spirit of life to enter her body. From that hour she was made whole; and we all felt to praise the name of God."

Phoebe tells her side of the story:

When she died, she saw her body lying upon the bed, the sisters weeping. She remembered looking at them, at Wilford, and her baby.

> While gazing upon this scene, two persons came into the room. . . . One of these messengers said to her that she might have her choice—she might go to rest in the spirit world, or, upon one condition, she could have the privilege of returning to her tabernacle and of continuing her labors upon the earth. The condition was that if she felt she could stand by her husband, and with him pass through all the cares, trials, tribulations, and afflictions of life which he would be called upon to pass through for the gospel's sake unto the end, she might return.

Phoebe looked again at her husband and child and thought about what they would have to go through, and then said, "Yes, I will do it."

It was at that moment when Wilford was moved by the Spirit to administer to Phoebe.[11]

11. Matthias F. Cowley, *Wilford Woodruff: His Life and Labors* (Snowy River Ventures, 2010), 97.

89 He Begged Those in Charge to Let Him Return

Don and Rosemary Bloomfield were married before he left his home in New Mexico to fight in World War II. Don was ordered to the Philippines. In 1942, the Japanese army conquered that land and took more than 78,000 US soldiers prisoner.

For more than three years, Don suffered immensely in a Japanese prisoner of war camp. Thousands of American soldiers died from malaria, lack of food, poor nutrition, extreme cold, or the brutal treatment of their captors.

Don worked in the POW camp shoveling and carrying coal, in spite of being constantly sick.

After contracting malaria, Don actually died. His body was taken to a tent where they kept the dead.

Don later told his family that when he went to the spirit world "he begged those in charge to let him return to life long enough to bring his body back to the States and be able to see his loved ones once more."

The next thing Don remembers was walking out of the "dead tent." A Japanese guard said to him, "What are you doing here? You're dead."

Don's only reply was, "I'm not dead."

After the United States dropped two atomic bombs on Japan, the Japanese surrendered. Prisoners of war were soon allowed to return to their homes.

Don was joyfully reunited with Rosemary, but his health had been ruined forever. He died a little over a year after returning home. Rosemary gave birth to a baby girl just six weeks later.[12]

---

12. *Saints at War: Experiences of Latter-day Saints in World War II*, Edited by Robert C. Freeman and Dennis G. Wright (Salt Lake City: Covenant Communications, 2001), 270–80.

Although rare, I testify that these kinds of miracles still happen today. Our Heavenly Father, the creator of life, has the power to give life again—if He so wills. At times, He will inspire righteous men to use the Holy Priesthood they bear to call back the dead. I pray that I may always be worthy to listen and act, if that time ever comes.

Chapter 11

"Special" Miracles

"And God wrought special miracles by the hands of Paul."
Acts 19:11

90 Robert Heard a Distinct Voice Whisper a Name

Seriously ill with tuberculosis, Robert Snyder had spent three years confined to his bedroom. He spent most of his time studying and pondering the Bible.

One night while in prayer, Robert heard a distinct voice whisper a name—John E. Page. Who was John E. Page? He had never heard of the man before, and what did John E. Page have to do with him?

Two weeks later, two missionaries from The Church of Jesus Christ of Latter-day Saints preached near his home. Robert's sister was soon converted and baptized. He asked his sister the names of the missionaries. One of them was John E. Page.

Soon Robert was also baptized and received the gift of the Holy Ghost. The disease he was told was incurable immediately left him. He later served for five years as a missionary himself, baptizing hundreds of people.[1]

A DIFFERENT KIND OF MIRACLE

Some miracles don't fit into a particular category, they are unique. Perhaps that is why Luke wrote, "God wrought *special miracles* by the hands of Paul" (Acts 19:11, emphasis added). I like the designation "special miracles" better than leftover stories because they truly are special. So, sit back and enjoy these incredible true incidents in the lives of people like you and me.

91 *Not Enough Bread*

It poured rain in the Philippines on the first Sunday in September 1989. Sacrament meeting in the Cadiz Ward began at 9:00 a.m. Only five people sat in the chapel when the meeting began; it was not easy for members who lived far away to come when it was raining.

A few more people came as the opening hymn was sung. During announcements, more people drifted in. By the time the sacrament hymn began, at least one hundred people were in attendance, far more than those who had prepared the sacrament had expected.

The two men assigned to administer the sacrament looked worried. When the hymn was completed, one of them kneeled to offer the blessing on the bread. For some reason, he did not immediately rise after the prayer; his head remained bowed, as if still in prayer. The sacrament trays were handed to the Aaronic Priesthood holders; the young men also looked concerned.

After both the sacrament bread and water had been passed to the congregation, a member of the ward bishopric bore his testimony of the gospel. He then invited the congregation to do the same. Members of The Church of Jesus Christ of

1. Leonard J. Arrington and Susan Arrington Madsen, *Sun-Bonnet Sisters: True Stories of Mormon Women and Frontier Life* (Salt Lake City: Bookcraft, 1984), 34–35.

Latter-day Saints call this a "Fast and Testimony" meeting. It is usually held on the first Sunday of every month.

The first person to come to the pulpit was one of the men who had blessed the sacrament. He spoke of the great love God has for all His children.

His companion at the sacrament table followed him. In an emotional voice, he told of the miracle they had witnessed that day. He explained that the bishop had brought only two small rolls of bread for the sacrament; because of the rains, he had expected only a handful of people to attend church. Then the members flooded in.

"The two men administering the sacrament knew that no matter how they broke the bread, there wasn't going to be enough. So, after the sacrament prayer, they said another prayer and told the Lord there were only about 40 pieces of bread to serve 100 people or more. They asked for divine intervention."

As the bread was passed to the congregation, the two brethren watched carefully as every person desiring to do so partook of the sacrament—there was enough for all.

Tears filled everyone's eyes and they sat in silence. The Spirit was so strong that nobody wanted to break the silence. Finally, the Bishop stood and said, "With God, nothing is impossible. Heavenly Father moves in mysterious ways to bestow blessings on His children."[2]

92 *Three Coins in a Catfish*

The New Testament book of Matthew records one of the more unusual miracles of the Savior. The tax collector had come calling, and Peter expressed his concern to Jesus. Jesus told Peter, a fisherman by trade, to go down to the Sea of Galilee, cast a hook, and bring up the first fish. Peter did so, and when he opened the mouth of the fish there was a coin—enough to pay the taxes for both Peter and Jesus (Matthew 17:24–27).

2. Evelyn B. Caesar, "Not Enough Bread," *Ensign*, Apr. 2004, 68–69.

A similar miracle occurred in the latter days. The Latter-day Saints first came to Independence, Jackson County, Missouri in 1831; it was just a frontier town then. Most of the residents were from the southern, slave-owning states and had very different beliefs and practices from members of The Church of Jesus Christ coming from New York and Ohio.

There was a tentative peace for a time while both sides established homes, farms, and businesses, but the inevitable conflict came in 1833. An unruly mob forced the Latter-day Saints from their homes in November. They fled north to the Missouri River and ferried across to Clay County where the citizens were more sympathetic to the plight of the Mormons.

However, some families could not afford the fee to ride the ferry across. The mobs had threatened to kill any who remained behind. What could they do?

Some of the stranded men decided to try to catch fish and hoped to sell them to the ferry operators for passage across the mighty river. They put their fishing lines out in the evening. When they brought their lines back in the next day, they found two or three small fish and a huge catfish weighing fourteen pounds.

When they gutted the catfish, they were astonished to find three bright silver half dollars, just the amount needed to pay for ferrying their teams over the river. This miracle caused great rejoicing among the Saints.[3]

93 *The Book That Would Not Burn*

Two missionaries knocked at the door of a large white house in Gallup, New Mexico. A woman answered the door and invited them in. They taught her about the Book of Mormon and asked her to read and pray about it. However, she could not read. She asked the missionaries if she could keep the book anyway since she had accumulated an impressive library for her children; she wanted them to read and appreciate books. The two young

3. Mary Elizabeth Rollins Lightner, *Utah Genealogical and Historical Magazine*, July 1926, 197.

missionaries gladly gave her the Book of Mormon and planned to return soon to teach the family about the gospel.

Unfortunately, the missionaries were transferred out of the area.

About a year later, Elder Ervin Lynn was transferred back to Gallup, New Mexico, but with a different companion. He was excited to return to the big white house to teach the woman and her family more about the Book of Mormon. To his surprise, there was no longer a big white house; there was nothing but ashes and blackened metal.

Upon inquiry, Elder Lynn learned that her family had moved to another part of the state after their house was destroyed by fire. He also learned about a miracle in connection with the fire.

When fire fighters arrived at the house, it was nearly consumed by flames. They told the family they could not save anything. The mother pleaded with them to save her library, so the firemen turned their hoses to that area, but it was in vain.

Several days later, family members stirred through the ashes. "There, perfectly undisturbed by fire or water, was the copy of the Book of Mormon that I had given the family. The other books had been burned to ashes."

Elder Lynn was able to find the woman's new address and wrote to her about the protection of her Book of Mormon. "I told her that I felt the Lord had preserved this book, because she didn't know how to read, to let her know of its truthfulness. She eventually received a testimony and was baptized along with members of her family."

Years later, Ervin Lynn visited her in New Mexico, and she showed him the undamaged copy of the Book of Mormon. The family has since remained active, and many have filled missions for the Church."[4]

4. Ervin Lynn, "The Book That Would Not Burn," *Ensign,* Oct. 1986, 61–62.

94 Look, It's the Only Book Not Burnt

A similar, more recent story took place in the Philippines in 2015. Sister Kalonihea loved serving in the Tacloban mission because there were so many opportunities for service. The missionaries cleaned and fixed up homes, tended crops, and even helped to extinguish fires.

One hot afternoon, Sister Kalonihea and her companion Sister Dumas were having lunch in their apartment when they saw smoke in a nearby neighborhood; the smoke was thick and black.

Immediately, they rushed from their apartment to help. Two houses were on fire and the fire department did not have enough water to extinguish both.

Sister Kalonihea said, "We just knew they needed our help, so we filled up buckets with water. There were people everywhere scrambling to help put out the fire."

After the fire was extinguished, the missionaries located the family to offer their assistance. "They were all just heart-broken to see their home burned and wondered why God would allow this to happen."

It then occurred to Sister Kalonihea that they had visited this same house the previous week. At that time, the family said they were not interested in listening to the missionaries.

Seeing their great need, Sister Kalonihea and Sister Dumas insisted on helping in the cleanup. They started handwashing their clothes—filthy from ashes and smoke.

Suddenly, one of the family members called them to look at something.

"What we saw was amazing," said Sister Kalonihea. Sandwiched in with a pile of ashes and burned books was a blue copy of The Book of Mormon—practically untouched.

The man who had found it said, "Look, look, it's the only book that's not burnt, and look it's not even wet."

The family recognized this miracle as a sign from God that they needed to listen to the gospel message. The sisters began teaching the family, and the entire family was soon baptized members of The Church of Jesus Christ of Latter-day Saints. They knew that losing their home "may have been the only way to find their new home and eternal place with God."[5]

95 "The Stars Shall Fall from Heaven"

October 5, 1833, the Prophet Joseph Smith made a remarkable prophecy: "Forty days shall not pass, and the stars shall fall from heaven."

Several of those in attendance were not members of the Church. One of them was already very skeptical about this so-called "prophet." He wrote the prophecy on a piece of paper and thought to himself, "*This will prove Joseph Smith a false prophet.*"

Thirty-nine days later, two men were hunting in the woods and got lost. Night had fallen and they sought shelter at the home of this same skeptic. He let them in, and upon finding that they were Latter-day Saints, showed them the prophecy of Joseph Smith. He exultingly asked what they thought of their prophet now.

One of the men, Joseph Hancock, calmly replied, "There is one night left of the time, and if Joseph said so, the stars will certainly fall tonight. This prophecy will all be fulfilled."

November 12–13, 1833, was known to all the world as "The Night of the Falling Stars." Astronomers have verified the date as a spectacular appearance of the Leonid meteor shower. One man calculated that as many as 240,000 meteors might have been visible that single night in 1833.

Parley P. Pratt remembered it well:

> To our great astonishment all the firmament seemed enveloped in splendid fireworks, as if every star in the broad expanse had been hurled from its course. . . . Thousands of bright meteors were shooting through space in every direction, with long trains of light following their course.

5. "Conversion Story: The Book of Mormon Was The Only Book That Was Spared From Fire," the Moroni Channel, June 27, 2016, https://www.moronichannel.org/stories/conversion/conversion-story-the-book-of-mormon-was-the-only-book-that-was-spared-from-fire/.

> This lasted for several hours and was only closed by the rising sun. Every heart was filled with joy at this majestic display of signs and wonders.[6]

Someone finally awoke Joseph Smith about 4:00 a.m. After viewing the marvelous display, he wrote, "In the midst of this shower of fire, I was led to exclaim, 'How marvelous are thy works, O Lord! I thank Thee for Thy mercy unto Thy servant.'"[7]

And what of the skeptic who first doubted the prophecy? The two hunters who had stayed the night at his house called him out to witness the spectacular display in the heavens. The man turned "pale as death and spoke not a word."[8] He became very friendly to the Latter-day Saints after that, and he even asked the prophet to come to his house. Joseph did so, and they discussed the restored Church of Jesus Christ at length, but the man was not known to have ever joined the Church.

Remember what was said in an earlier chapter: faith must come first. Miracles do not produce faith.

96 *They Only Speak French*

"Hey, guys! Come back!" the man's voice called out.

Christina Earhart turned and saw two small boys running across the store parking lot. They were obviously upset; she could see them crying. The Spirit whispered to her, "You can be of help here." The message was so clear that she found herself running toward the boys.

She knelt beside the older boy and said, "Hi. My name is Christina. Are you OK?"

He began crying even harder. The salesman from the store joined her. "I think they only speak French," he said. "We just found them running through the store, lost."

Christina had spoken French as a child before being adopted by an English-speaking family, but her French was very poor.

---

6. Parley P. Pratt, *Autobiography of Parley P. Pratt* (Chicago: Law, King & Law, 1888), 82–84.
7. Joseph Smith, Journal, Nov. 13, 1833, in *Joseph Smith Papers,* J1:16–17.
8. Philo Dibble, "Recollections of the Prophet Joseph Smith," *Juvenile Instructor,* 27:23.

She repeated her introduction in French. As she spoke comfort to the boys, her words came clearly and smoothly.

Hearing Christina speak his native tongue, the older boy spoke very rapidly telling her that he and his brother were lost and had not been able to find their parents in the store, so they had come running outside to look for them. As she listened, she was amazed that she could not only speak French freely, but that she could understand every word he was saying.

"They've lost their parents and want to wait for them here at their car," she told the salesman. The boy told Christina the names of their parents and the salesman had them paged in the store. A few minutes later the family was reunited.

As Christina joined them, she suddenly found that she could no longer speak any more French. The boys could no longer understand anything she said. She finally resorted back to English, "Bye. It was nice to meet you."

Christina went to her car, expressing her gratitude to her Heavenly Father for using her in a time of need. "I was humbled that the Lord could magnify my limited abilities to fulfill His purposes. I was grateful to witness what can happen as we offer ourselves to Him when called upon, even in the most unlikely of settings."[9]

97 *Miracle at the Alpine Slide*

While Merlene Featherstone watched her son take his children down the Alpine slide near Park City, Utah, she saw a woman searching for something in the grass. Merlene walked over and asked if she could help. The woman replied in heavily accented English that she was looking for the lens cap to her camera. Merlene knelt and assisted her in the search.

She said, "You're not from the United States. Are you from Mexico?"

"No, I'm from Ecuador."

9. Christina Albrecht Earhart, "The Spirit Whispered to Me," *Ensign,* Apr. 2015.

That's interesting, Merlene thought to herself, *my son Joseph served his mission in Ecuador twenty years ago*. She said out loud, "What are you doing here from Ecuador?"

"I have come to find the beloved missionary who baptized me into the Church. I will love him as long as time lasts."

"How long ago were you baptized?"

"About 20 years ago."

What a coincidence, Merlene mused. "We have a son who served about 20 years ago in Ecuador. I'll bet he'll know him. What was the elder's name?"

"Well, it was a peculiar name: Elder Joseph Featherstone."

Merlene couldn't believe it. "Come on over to the bottom of the slide. I want to introduce you to someone."

As he came to the end of the slide, Joseph saw his mother standing next to a woman. As he approached them, he suddenly recognized her. They ran into each other's arms, weeping for joy.[10]

Just a coincidence? What about the other stories in this chapter? Just coincidences?

10. Vaughn J. Featherstone, "Things Too Wonderful for Me," Brigham Young University devotional, Feb. 13, 2001, speeches.byu.edu.

Chapter 12

When Miracles Don't Happen

"If they die they shall die unto me."
Doctrine and Covenants 42:44

This chapter has been difficult for me to write, but I have felt compelled to write about why miracles don't always happen. If I truly believe, and I do, that miracles happen, I must also be prepared to explain why they don't. Even when faith is strong, prayers are earnest, and reasons seem so compelling, miracles sometimes don't happen.

The picture above shows three of my grandchildren at the grave of my first wife, Vickie Church Woodstock. I can't begin to number the prayers that were offered on her behalf by her children, grandchildren, brothers and sisters, aunts and uncles, friends, coworkers, ward members, mother, and husband. How many priesthood blessings had she received? How many times had her name been placed on temple prayer rolls?

After Vickie was flown by Life Flight to the Huntsman Cancer Center in Salt Lake City, I received word that all our children and grandchildren were having a special fast on her behalf; our ten grandchildren at that time ranged in age from twelve down to two. I began to weep and cried out, "How can the Lord not hear the fasting and prayers of these little children?"

A few months after Vickie died, on a Sunday evening, I turned on my television and watched the Church Educational System devotional for young adults. I was still teaching at the Cedar City Institute of Religion and wanted to discuss the devotional with my students the next day.

The speaker was Elder David A. Bednar of the Council of the Twelve Apostles. As he spoke, I felt as if he were speaking directly to me. His topic: Accepting the Lord's Will and Timing.

Elder Bednar told of an experience he had with a young couple he called John and Heather. Just three weeks after their marriage and sealing in the Salt Lake temple, John was diagnosed with bone cancer. He was given only a 30% chance of survival.

For the next four months, John underwent chemotherapy treatments and an operation on his leg to remove a cancerous tumor. "The treatments caused me to be sicker than I had ever been in my life. I lost my hair, dropped 41 pounds, and my body felt like it was falling apart. The chemotherapy also affected me emotionally, mentally, and spiritually. Life was a roller coaster. . . . But through it all, [Heather] and I maintained the faith that God would heal me. We just knew it."

John received several priesthood blessings throughout his ordeal, including from his father, his father-in-law, and his mission president.

One day, apostle David A. Bednar visited John and Heather in the hospital. Elder Bednar talked about the time he had met John on his mission, his subsequent marriage, and the trials and sufferings they had undergone since.

John asked Elder Bednar to give him a priesthood blessing. "I was sure that since Elder Bednar was an apostle, he would bless the elements of my body to realign, and I would jump out of the bed and start to dance."

Heather's thoughts were similar: "I was convinced that Elder Bednar would place his hands on [John's] head and completely heal him of the cancer. I knew that through the power of the priesthood he could be healed, and I wanted so bad for that to happen."

Elder Bednar said he would be glad to give John a priesthood blessing, but first he needed to ask some questions.

Elder Bednar later recalled, "I then posed questions I had not planned to ask and had never previously considered: "[John], do you have the faith not to be healed? If it is the will of our Heavenly Father that you are transferred by death in your youth to the spirit world to continue your ministry, do you have the faith to submit to His will and not be healed?"

Heather was at first terrified that she could lose her newlywed husband. John said, "Having the faith not to be healed seemed counterintuitive; but that perspective changed the way my wife and I thought and allowed us to put our trust fully in the Father's plan for us. We learned we needed to gain the faith that the Lord is in charge whatever the outcome may be. . . . As we prayed, our petitions changed from 'Please make me whole' to 'Please give me faith to accept whatever outcome Thou hast planned for me.'"[1]

SOMETIMES, THE ANSWER IS NO

President Dallin H. Oaks said, "Miracles are not available for the asking. . . . The will of the Lord is always paramount. The priesthood of the Lord cannot be used to work a miracle contrary to the will of the Lord."[2]

My friend and former seminary teacher, Brent Farley, shared the following personal experience. One morning, he received a phone call from a member of his ward.

"Bishop, this is Brother Olson. Can you come up right away? My son has passed away."

"I'm on my way."

1. David A. Bednar, "That We Might 'Not . . . Shrink,'" Church Educational Systems fireside, University of Texas Arlington, March 3, 2013.
2. Dallin H. Oaks, "Miracles," *Ensign*, June 2001.

Bishop Farley quickly left for the Olson's home. "As I entered, I saw Sister Olson in the living room, beside herself with grief. He led me up the stairs and into the bedroom of the child. It was obvious at a glance that the child was beyond revival."

"Bishop," said Brother Olson, "can we use the power of the priesthood to call him back to life?"

In general, the answer to that question is yes. Priesthood power can raise the dead; I gave several examples in chapter ten. But the first question that should be asked is: what is the will of the Lord?

Bishop Farley said to the grieving father, "I don't know, but I'll ask."

He knelt near the crib and began, "Heavenly Father, this faithful brother has asked me a question as his bishop. I cannot answer regarding life and death, but Thou canst. If it be thy will to give permission, I know that the power of the priesthood can bring this child back to life. May we give him such a blessing?"

Bishop Farley received a direct impression: "No."

He turned toward Brother Olson and shook his head. He understood and accepted the will of the Lord.[3]

While serving in the First Presidency of The Church of Jesus Christ of Latter-day Saints, President Marion G. Romney said, "We mortals, in exercising the priesthood, do not do so in our own right as Jesus did. The priesthood we hold is a delegated power. We can only exercise it within the limits the Lord has set, upon the conditions he has specified, and in his name."[4]

Let me tell you a little about President Marion George Romney. He was born in Colonia Juárez, Mexico, and married Ida Jensen in the Salt Lake temple in 1924. Their first two children died in infancy. George and Ida pleaded with the Lord for children. He spoke about their wrestle with the Lord in a later conference of the Church:

> We set about through fasting and prayer to obtain it. We considered many of the scriptures which seemed to make a blanket promise that "Whatsoever ye shall ask in prayer, believing, ye shall receive." (Matthew 21:22.) We asked, we

3. S. Brent Farley, *Spiritually Yours: Applying Gospel Principles for Personal Progression* (Bountiful, UT: Horizon Publishers & Distributors, 1982), 11–12.
4. Marion G. Romney, "Priesthood," *Ensign,* May 1982, 43.

> believed, we thought we had faith, but though we fasted often and prayed fervently, the years rolled by without bringing us the desired answer to our prayers. Finally, we concluded that we had not fully understood somehow—that we were concentrating our faith and prayers upon receiving the particular thing, which by predetermination we had set our hearts upon. We had to reconsider the conditions of the promise. We found that Jesus had stated them in full to the Nephites as follows: "Whatsoever ye shall ask the Father in my name, *which is right*, believing that ye shall receive, behold it shall be given unto you" (3 Nephi 18:20), and to this generation thus, "Whatsoever ye ask the Father in my name it shall be given unto you, *that is expedient for you*." (D&C 88:64.) We had to learn to be as earnest in praying "if it be Thy will," as we were when presenting our personal desires and appeals. We have no need to fear that our well-being will not be served by such an approach.[5]

With this background into President Romney's faith and testimony, let me share a miracle that he experienced later in his life.

98 "It Is Not Contrary to My Will"

In 1967, after 43 years of marriage, President Marion G. Romney's beloved wife, Ada, suffered a serious stroke. The doctors told him that the bleeding in her brain was severe. She could be kept alive through artificial means, but the doctors offered little hope for recovery.

President Romney anguished over his dying wife and companion. He gave her a priesthood blessing, but he was "reluctant to counsel the Lord about the matter because of his earlier unsuccessful experience of praying that he and Ida might have children; he knew that he could never ask in prayer for something which was not in harmony with the will of the Lord."

5. Marion G. Romney, address delivered at Salt Lake Institute of Religion, Oct. 18, 1974, 8–9.

Ida continued to decline. Marion fasted and prayed that he could show the Lord his faith, "and that he would accept God's will in their lives."

One evening, after visiting Ida in the hospital and seeing her unable to speak or recognize him, he returned to his home feeling depressed. He turned to the scriptures for comfort. He opened his bookmark in the Book of Mormon and read verses he had read numerous times before, but this time it seemed as if the Lord was speaking directly to him:

> Blessed art thou, [Marion], for those things which thou hast done; for I have beheld how thou hast with unwearyingness declared the word, which I have given unto thee, unto this people. And thou hast not feared them, and hast not sought thine own life, but hast sought my will, and to keep my commandments.
>
> And now, because thou hast done this with such unwearyingness, behold, I will bless thee forever; and I will make thee mighty in word and in deed, in faith and in works; yea, even that all things shall be done unto thee according to thy word, for thou shalt not ask that which is contrary to my will (Helaman 10:4–5).

"There was the answer. He had sought only to know and obey the will of the Lord, and the Lord had spoken. He fell to his knees and poured out his heart, and as he concluded his prayer with the phrase, 'Thy will be done,' he either felt or actually heard a voice which said, 'It is not contrary to my will that Ida be healed.'"

President Romney immediately dressed and drove to the hospital. It was almost three o'clock in the morning. He laid his hands on her head and "invoked the power of the priesthood in her behalf. He pronounced a simple blessing and then uttered the incredible promise that she would recover her health and mental powers and yet perform a great mission upon the earth."

Ida opened her eyes and said, "For goodness' sake, Marion, what are you doing here?"

He sat next to her on the bed and said, "Ida, how are you?"

"Compared to what, Marion? Compared to what?" She had not lost her sense of humor.

Ida Romney soon left the hospital. Seven years later on April 6, 1974, she raised her arm to the square, along with the entire membership of the Church, to sustain Marion George Romney as second counselor in the First Presidency of The Church of Jesus Christ of Latter-day Saints—"a great mission upon the earth" indeed.[6]

GOD'S PERSPECTIVE

Perspective is the way we see things. Anyone who has dealt with small children know they have limited perspective. To a two-year old, the entire world revolves around them. Part of growing up is to gain a larger view of the world and how we each fit in.

Adults have problems with perspective too. They don't always see things from a larger viewpoint. Sometimes, all they see is their own problems, pain, and suffering. All of us sometimes need to step back and look at the big picture. I know that is hard to do when we are so close to painful situations. But therein lies the problem—we are too close. Trust Heavenly Father that He can see better than you. The Lord told the prophet Isaiah, "For my thoughts are not your thoughts, neither are your ways my ways . . .. For as the heavens are higher than the earth, so are my ways higher than your ways, and my thoughts than your thoughts" (Isaiah 55:8–9).

Ultimately, the big picture is encompassed in our Heavenly Father's plan of salvation. He sent us to earth to obtain a physical body. He knew that because we came to a fallen world, it would not be easy. We would have pain and suffering, and eventually our physical bodies would die, and we would return to His presence. But that is the point. Heavenly Father *wants us to die.* He wants us to return to Him. It was never His intention for us to remain on earth forever. Why? Because He has something better in mind. Not just better, but so extraordinary and beautiful, we can't even begin to imagine it. "Eye

6. F. Burton Howard, *Marion* G. *Romney: His Life and Faith* (Salt Lake City: Bookcraft, 1988), 137–42.

hath not seen, nor ear heard, neither have entered into the heart of man, the things which God hath prepared for them that love him (1 Corinthians 2:9).

The big picture I am trying to paint for you is that death is not evil. President Russell M. Nelson taught, "We start to die the moment we are born. Why? The reason is simple. Our Heavenly Father wants us to return to him. He gave us life, and He provided the means by which we could return to Him. Viewed from an eternal perspective, we live to die; and we die to live again."[7]

99 *In Keeping with God's Will*

Even righteous men and women need to be reminded of eternal perspectives. Just before he was called as an apostle, Marriner W. Merrill served as president of the Logan, Utah temple. His oldest son, named after him, and the manager of his business interests during his full-time service to the Lord, suddenly died, leaving a large family of small children. President Merrill was heartbroken and refused to be comforted.

One day he was traveling from the temple to his home, still grieving over the unexpected loss of his son. He sat in his carriage, deep in contemplation and sorrow, when he suddenly noticed that his horse had stopped in the middle of the road.

Looking up, he saw his deceased son standing in the road beside the carriage. His son said, "Father, you are mourning my departure unduly. You are overconcerned about my family and their welfare. I have much work to do and your grieving gives me much concern. I am in a position to render effective service to my family. You should take comfort, for you know there is much work to be done here and it was necessary for me to be called. You know that the Lord doeth all things well."

He left as suddenly as he appeared, but from that moment on, Elder Marriner Merrill was comforted knowing "that the death of his son was in keeping with God's will."[8]

---

7. Russell M. Nelson, *The Gateway We Call Death* (Salt Lake City: Deseret Book, 1995), 5.
8. Bryant S. Hinckley, *The Faith of Our Pioneer Fathers* (Salt Lake City: Deseret Book, 1956), 182–83.

Elder Merrill's experience with his son reminds me of these words from President Spencer W. Kimball: "If we look at mortality as a complete existence, then pain, sorrow and a short life could be a calamity. But if we look upon the whole of life in its *eternal perspective* stretching far into the premortal past and into the eternal post-death future, then all happenings may have more meaning and may fall into proper place."[9]

Trusting that our Heavenly Father sees our mortal life from His "higher ways" will bring peace and comfort in all times, good and bad. Trust that He really does have our best interests at heart.

C. S. Lewis gave the following wonderful analogy:

> Imagine yourself as a living house. God comes in to rebuild that house. At first, perhaps, you can understand what He is doing. He is getting the drains right and stopping the leaks in the roof and so on; you knew that those jobs needed doing and so you are not surprised. But presently He starts knocking the house about in a way that hurts abominably and does not seem to make any sense. What on earth is He up to? The explanation is that He is building quite a different house from the one you thought of—throwing out a new wing here, putting on an extra floor there, running up towers, making courtyards. You thought you were being made into a decent little cottage: but He is building a palace. He intends to come and live in it Himself.[10]

THE TENDER MERCIES OF THE LORD

The prophet Nephi expressed his personal testimony of God's love in the first chapter of the Book of Mormon. In the middle of his narrative of his family's escape from Jerusalem, he states, "But behold, I, Nephi, will show unto you that the tender mercies of the Lord are over all those whom he hath chosen, because of their faith, to make them mighty even unto the power of deliverance" (1 Nephi 1:20).

---

9. Spencer W. Kimball, *Tragedy or Destiny*, Speeches of the Year (Provo, Utah: Brigham Young University Press, 1955), 2, emphasis added.
10. C. S. Lewis, *Mere Christianity* (Macmillan, 1960), 160.

Many times, when miracles don't happen, we will feel "the tender mercies of the Lord" in our lives. These tender mercies are expressions from our loving and kind Heavenly Father that He knows and cares about our personal situations.

Such a tender mercy came to a little girl dying of cancer. It was not Heavenly Father's will that a miracle of healing take place, but He did send a miracle.

100 *I Just Knew You Would Come*

Christal Methvin was just ten years old when she died in 1974. She had one wish before passing—to receive a priesthood blessing from Elder Thomas S. Monson of the Quorum of the Twelve Apostles.

The Methvin family owned a ranch eighty miles from Shreveport in northwest Louisiana. Christal loved to ride horses and was active in the local 4-H club. When a lump was found on her leg, her parents took her to a specialist in New Orleans. The diagnosis was cancer. She had surgery and soon recovered, but the cancer spread to her lungs.

The Methvin family made plans to fly to Salt Lake City to receive a blessing from a general authority of The Church of Jesus Christ of Latter-day Saints. This was a time when the Church was still small, and the general authorities had more time in their schedule to receive individual callers at their office to give counsel and administer priesthood blessings. As the Church grew, members were encouraged to receive blessings from their local ward and stake leaders. After all, an eighteen-year-old elder has as much priesthood power as an apostle.

The Methvin family didn't personally know any general authorities of the Church, so they showed Christal a recent picture of the leaders of the Church and let her choose whom she would like to bless her. She pointed at Elder Thomas S. Monson.

Unfortunately, Christal's condition worsened and she was unable to make the flight to Salt Lake City. Her faith was such that she said to her parents, "Isn't stake conference approaching?

Isn't a general authority assigned? And why not Brother Monson? If I can't go to him, the Lord can send him to me."

At that time, general authorities were given their travel schedules well in advance, and someone else had been assigned to the Shreveport, Louisiana Stake. Elder Thomas S. Monson had been assigned to the El Paso, Texas stake conference over 800 miles away.

But the first of two miracles happened. The president of the council of the twelve called Elder Monson to his office and told him he wanted to send a different apostle to El Paso. President Ezra Taft Benson then said, "Brother Monson, I feel impressed to have you visit the Shreveport Louisiana Stake." Neither men knew anything of Christal Methvin.

Elder Monson's schedule was filled with meetings on the day he arrived in Shreveport. "Rather apologetically, Stake President Charles F. Cagle asked if my schedule would permit me time to provide a blessing to a ten-year-old girl afflicted with cancer."

Elder Monson told President Cagle that he would be happy to do it but wondered looking at their busy schedule when they would have time. He asked, "Would she be at the conference, or was she in a local Shreveport hospital?"

President Cagle quietly answered that Christal was confined to her home—more than eighty miles away.

Elder Monson saw no possible time in their schedule and suggested, "Could we not remember the little one in our public prayers at conference? Surely the Lord would understand."

The Methvin family understood but was disappointed. They knew that the Lord had brought Elder Monson to Shreveport for stake conference. Could He not bring him to their home? At 7:45 p.m., the family knelt in prayer and implored Heavenly Father that Christal could have her last wish granted.

Eighty miles away, Elder Thomas S. Monson was seated on the rostrum in the chapel getting ready to address the congregation. The time on the wall clock read 7:45. Elder Monson later testified, "I was sorting my notes, preparing to step to the pulpit, when I heard a voice speak to my spirit. The message was brief, the words familiar: 'Suffer the little children to come unto me, and forbid them not: for of such is the kingdom of God' (Mark 10:14). My notes became a blur. My thoughts turned to a tiny girl in need of a blessing."

Elder Monson turned to Bishop James Serra, also sitting on the rostrum, and asked him to leave the meeting and notify the Methvins that Elder Monson would be coming early the next morning to bless Christal. The phone rang as the Methvin family rose from prayer.

Elder Monson said, "I shall ever remember and never forget that early-morning journey to a heaven the Methvin family calls home. I have been in hallowed places—even holy houses—but never have I felt more strongly the presence of the Lord than in the Methvin home. Christal looked so tiny lying peacefully on such a large bed. The room was bright and cheerful. The sunshine from the east window filled the bedroom with light as the Lord filled our hearts with love."

The visitors gathered around her bedside and "gazed down at a child who was too ill to rise—almost too weak to speak. Her illness had now rendered her sightless. So strong was the spirit that I fell to my knees, took her frail hand in mine, and said simply, 'Christal, I am here.' She parted her lips and whispered, 'Brother Monson, I just knew you would come.' I looked around the room. No one was standing. Each was on bended knee. A blessing was given. A faint smile crossed Christal's face. Her whispered 'thank you' provided an appropriate benediction. Quietly, each filed from the room." Christal died four days later.[11]

11. Thomas S. Monson, "The Faith of a Child," *Ensign*, Oct. 1975, 31.

DOUBT YOUR DOUBTS BEFORE YOU DOUBT YOUR FAITH

When hoped-for miracles don't materialize, it doesn't mean Heavenly Father doesn't love you. You are His child. Try to remember that this earth is only our temporary abode. He wants us to return to His home and live in eternal glory.

I must confess that there were times during my wife's illness and death that I doubted. I doubted my faith in God, my belief in His plan, and His love for me. During this time of difficulty, I heard Elder Dieter F. Uchtdorf say, "Doubt your doubts before you doubt your faith."[12] For some reason, that gave me the encouragement I needed to hold on.

12. Dieter F. Uchtdorf, "Come, Join with Us," *Ensign,* Nov. 2013, 23.

Conclusion

The 100 latter-day miracles contained in this book are not just stories; they are real experiences that happened to real people. They are a witness that "God has not ceased to be a God of miracles" (Mormon 9:15).

Miracles happen all around us every day. "Those miracles we hear strengthen our faith; they bear witness to us again and again that God loves us, that he is concerned, that he will, when necessary, *directly* influence our lives."[1]

"Just a Coincidence?" was the working title of this book when I first began it many years ago. After writing about each experience, I would ask the reader, "Was it just a coincidence?" I hope that as you have read these 100 miracles, you have come to the same conclusion I did—these were not coincidences. They were not somehow accidental. Elder Neal A. Maxwell said, "[C]oincidence is not an appropriate word to describe the workings of an omniscient God. He does not do things by 'coincidence' but instead by 'divine design.'"[2]

CAUTION

Jesus performed many miracles during His earthy ministry. I have always been surprised as I read the Holy Bible that not everyone who

1. Jay Parry, "Miracles Today?" *Ensign,* Jan. 1978.
2. Neal A. Maxwell, "Brim with Joy," Brigham Young University devotional, Jan. 23, 1996, speeches.byu.edu.

saw Jesus's miracles believed. "But though he had done so many miracles before them, yet they believed not on him" (John 12:37).

Why? The most obvious reason to me is lack of faith. Jesus told His Nephite disciples in America that amongst the Jews, "I could not show them so great miracles, because of their unbelief" (3 Nephi 19:35). As I wrote several times in this book, faith must come first. I am sure there will be some who browse through this book and doubt every single miracle as either just a coincidence or simply not possible, because they have no faith.

How is faith increased? Faith and righteousness are inseparably connected. The more righteous you are, the more faith you will have. Those who strive to live the principles and commandments as found in the gospel of Jesus Christ will not only be able to more readily identify miracles around them every day, but will be recipients of them. "Miracles are always performed among people who have faith. . . . Faith and righteousness are the powers by which miracles are wrought."[3] The prophet Russell M. Nelson testified to the people of all the world, "As you choose to let God prevail in your lives, you will experience for yourselves that our God is 'a God of miracles.'"[4]

THE GREATEST MIRACLES

I anticipate someone reading this book and asking, "Which is the greatest miracle?" My answer would be, "I have not written about the greatest miracles in this book." To me, the three greatest miracles are (1) the creation of this and countless other worlds, (2) the resurrection of Jesus Christ and our own subsequent resurrections, and (3) the changing of human hearts.

President Russell M. Nelson said, "The gift of the resurrection is the Lord's consummate act of healing. Thanks to Him, each body will be restored to its proper and perfect frame. Thanks to Him, no condition is hopeless. Thanks to Him, brighter days are ahead, both here and hereafter. Real joy awaits each of us."[5]

---

3. Bruce R. McConkie, *Mormon Doctrine,* 2nd ed. (Salt Lake City: Bookcraft, 1966), 507.
4. Russell N. Nelson, "Let God Prevail," *Ensign*, Nov. 2020, 95.
5. Russell N. Nelson, "Jesus Christ—the Master Healer," *Ensign*, Nov. 2005, 88.

President Dallin H. Oaks spoke to the young adults of The Church of Jesus Christ of Latter-day Saints about miracles. After recounting several latter-day miracles, he stated,

> But the greatest miracle is not in such things as restoring sight to the blind, healing an illness, or even raising the dead, since all of these restorations will happen, in any event, in the Resurrection . . . but an even greater miracle is a mighty change of heart by a son or daughter of God (see Mosiah 5:2). A change of heart, including new attitudes, priorities, and desires, is greater and more important than any miracle involving the body.

And then to make sure no one missed his point, he said, "I repeat, the body will be resurrected in any event, but a change affecting what the scriptures call the 'heart' of a spirit son or daughter of God is a change whose effect is eternal."[6]

My heart began to change in 1966 at the age of ten. A neighbor boy exemplified a true disciple of Jesus Christ by asking a very shy and lonely new move-in to play marbles with him and to attend Primary. At the same time, another disciple made friends with my mother and invited the missionaries to teach us. I will always remember feeling the Holy Ghost for the first time during our first meeting with the missionaries. My heart continues to change to this day. Every time I strive to be faithful, every time I study the scriptures, every time I read about inspirational miracles, my heart grows a little bit more.

TESTIMONY

"Miracles are one of the greatest evidences of the divinity of the Lord's work."[7] My faith in the reality and power of God, the Eternal Father, His son Jesus Christ, and in the Holy Ghost has increased with each miracle I have personally experienced or read about. I testify that the Godhead lives, and that they are involved in our lives "day by day" (Alma 37:40). May each of us "stand still, with the utmost assurance, to see the salvation of God, and for his arm to be revealed" (Doctrine and Covenants 123:17).

6. Dallin H. Oaks, "Miracles," *Ensign*, June 2001.
7. Bruce R. McConkie, *Mormon Doctrine*, 2nd ed. (Salt Lake City: Bookcraft, 1966), 507.

Notes

Notes

Notes

Notes

Notes

About the Author

Jonathan Woodstock is a retired educator with the Seminaries and Institutes of The Church of Jesus Christ of Latter-day Saints living in Arizona, Colorado, Utah, and Wyoming. After serving as a missionary in Vancouver, British Columbia, Canada, he completed his BA degree at Brigham Young University (1979). He later earned an MS degree from Utah State University (1986) and a PhD from the University of Wyoming (1998).

He was married for thirty-four years to Vickie Church Woodstock. She died of cancer in 2012. Together they had six children. In 2016, Jonathan met Amy Coombs on a dating website. They were married less than three months later. Together they taught English in China for a year with the BYU China Teacher Program.

Jonathan loves to play the piano, watch golf and football, and work on his family history. He also loves to serve his community and church, but most of all, he loves spending time with his family, which now consists of twenty grandchildren.